Y0-DKB-119

Bicycling Books®

THE MOST FREQUENTLY ASKED QUESTIONS ABOUT BICYCLING

by the editors of Bicycling® magazine

Compiled by:
Marcia Holoman

Contributions from:
John Schubert
Michael J. Kolin
Denise M. de la Rosa
Thom Lieb
Kathy Fones
Eugene A. Gaston, M.D.
David L. Smith, M.D.

Copyright © 1980 by Rodale Press, Inc.

All rights reserved. No part of this publication may be
reproduced or transmitted in any form or by any means,
electronic or mechanical, including photocopy, recording,
or any information storage and retrieval system without
the written permission of the publisher.

Printed in the United States of America on recycled paper,
containing a high percentage of de-inked fiber.

Book series design by K. A. Schell

Library of Congress Cataloging in Publication Data

Main entry under title:

The Most frequently asked questions about bicycling.

    (Bicycling books)
    1. Cycling—Miscellanea.　2. Bicycles and
tricycles—Miscellanea.　I. Holoman, Marcia.
II. Schubert, John, 1952–　　III. Bicycling (Emmaus,
Pa.)　IV. Series.
GV1043.7.M67　　796.6　　79-28685
ISBN 0-87857-300-3　paperback

2　4　6　8　10　9　7　5　3　1　paperback

Contents

Contents

Introduction

No doubt about it. Words get in the way. I recall a bike shop owner telling me about a fellow who stormed into his shop and demanded "one of those dohickeys for my gears." Trying to narrow the field a bit, the mechanic took the fellow over to a bike and started pointing out things: the shift levers, the chainwheel, the cogs, the front and rear derailleur, the cables. No luck.

After the shop owner pointed out almost all of the visible components on the bike, the man's eyes lit up with recognition. "That's it," he said, pointing to a brake pad. "One of those little black dohickeys for my gears." The bike mechanic wished he had world enough and time to explain the difference between gears and brakes.

I remember when I first got involved in cycling in a serious way (I wasn't serious; it was the other people). I went to a bicycle club meeting and the subject under discussion was an upcoming training ride. I might as well have been in another country. The club members were kicking around words like *freewheel sizes*, *wheelbase*, *fork rake*, *gearing up*, and *gearing down*. In no time at all I was lost. Of course, once on the ride it didn't take me long to learn the difference between a gear and a brake.

In some respects cycling is very much of a club activity; the sport has its own history, heroes, and language. Most of all, the sport has at its center the bike which is at once simple and difficult for many people. French-sounding words like *derailleur* are enough to confuse. And learning how to shift gears? That's something else.

At *Bicycling* magazine our phones are constantly ringing (and our mailboxes are constantly full) with basic questions about the bicycle and bicycling. The questions would fill a book: where do I

1

buy a bike; how do I know if a bike fits me; how do I ride a bike; how do I shift my 10-speed; how do I get into touring or racing; and so on. These are good questions. And for them, we think we have found good answers. In fact, you will find over 225 answers to the most frequently asked questions about bicycling. After you read this book you should have a good, fundamental knowledge of the bicycle and how to ride and repair it.

If you still have questions, visit your local bike shop.

James C. McCullagh
Editor/Publisher
Bicycling magazine

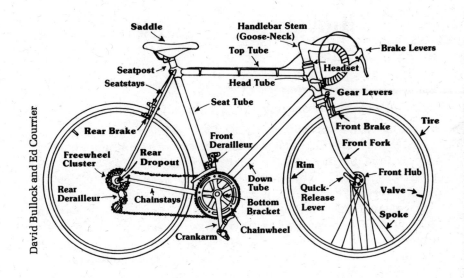

Bicycle parts guide.

David Bullock and Ed Courrier

Bicycling—the Sport

A. Can anyone bicycle?

Bicycling has no height, weight, or age restrictions. Cycling seems a natural for children, and there are many cyclists well up in years still capable of handling a bicycle and enjoying the sport.

B. Is a medical examination necessary before I begin cycling?

It is recommended that everyone first have a thorough physical examination by their doctor before starting any type of exercise program. Even if you are young, your cardiovascular system could possibly be out of shape if it is not accustomed to strenuous exercise. Also, people over 40 years old who have not had a long-term commitment to physical fitness may have an increased risk of heart attack or muscle damage. These people should not engage in strenuous exercise without a thorough medical evaluation and physical fitness training. Most important, once you have your doctor's approval, start out slowly in your exercise program. Your body needs time to acclimate itself to this new activity.

C. Why is bicycling a good form of exercise? How does it benefit me physically?

Bicycling is a form of exercise with which you can grow old. Physicians recommend this form of exercise, since the low-tension rhythmic factors have been shown by experiments to relieve the strains on the heart. Cycling also tends to maintain elasticity of the blood vessels and prevent hardening of the arteries and high blood pressure. It is a complete form of exercise—beneficial to your legs, arms, shoulders, back, diaphragm, and abdominal muscles. Cycling improves circulation, muscle tone, digestion, and weight control.

D. How often should I ride my bike each week to maintain fitness?

Twenty or 30 minutes per day would be enough to maintain cardiovascular tone and prevent loss of muscle tissue. The American

4

College of Sports Medicine makes the following recommendations for training to develop and maintain fitness:

1. Frequency of training—three to five days per week.
2. Intensity of training—60 to 90% of your maximum heart rate reserve (220, minus age in years, minus resting pulse rate).
3. Duration of training—15 to 60 minutes of continuous aerobic exercise.

E. What are the different types of riding?

Commuting, touring, racing, recreational riding, and errand running are your choices. Commuting on a bicycle is most rewarding when you pass long lines of traffic and jammed intersections. In addition to getting to work, you're getting valuable exercise.

Touring can set your spirit free. What better way is there to take in the sights and smells of the countryside? There are no limitations as to how far you can travel. With a little planning you can tour confidently from coast to coast or across the continents.

Bicycle racing is of growing interest in the United States. For years we took a back seat to the Europeans, whose support of bicycle racing is enormous. Sanctioned races are handled by the United States Cycling Federation. Velodromes (bicycle racing tracks) throughout the United States offer professional racing, as well as sponsoring grass-roots racing clubs. Other programs, such as the Open Bicycle Racing Association, give the novice a chance to race, and there are bicycle clubs in every state offering nonprofessional competition.

For the ecology minded, bicycling can be incorporated into weekend recreation or yearly vacation plans. For the economy minded, neighborhood jaunts and local errand running on a bicycle will save money every time.

F. I don't think I'd enjoy riding alone. What are my options?

Many cyclists prefer riding alone, enjoying the freedom of deciding their own destinations. Touring for a week or two, however, can get lonely, and a companion to share experiences can be very fulfilling. Bicycle touring clubs exist throughout the United States, offering diverse touring opportunities. There are even international cycle tours organized so that the beginner, as well as the experienced cyclist, can meet and share in a great experience.

G. I'm over 60 years of age and would not be able to handle a 10-speed bicycle. I would still like to ride a bike. What are my options?

Most folks over 60 would be able to handle a 10-speed bicycle but have convinced themselves that they cannot (never having ridden such a machine). If you are unwilling, unable, or, for whatever reason, skeptical of your capabilities on a 10-speed, there are several options.

Try a 5-speed or 3-speed bicycle. Those of you who are accustomed to the single-speed, coaster-brake models will delight in the performance of a geared bicycle. Remaining alternatives are the single speeds and adult tricycles. The tricycle may be just what you need to help build your confidence in handling a bicycle, or you might find it very satisfactory for your needs.

H. I'm interested in using my bike as transportation to and from work; however, I'm concerned about riding in heavy traffic. What should I do?

Bicycles and cars can mix well. Before you venture out into the streets, practice in an empty parking lot. Practice so you can start from a dead stop, and ride very slowly while toeing a straight line. Practice maneuvers like weaving between tin cans, looking behind you, while steering a straight line. Can you shift without looking? Once you have mastered these skills you are ready for the streets. Here are a few suggestions:

1. Be predictable. Follow the same rules of the road as a car driver.
2. Ride on the right-hand side of the right lane (with traffic).
3. Don't run stoplights or stop signs.
4. Remember to keep a check on traffic by looking over your left shoulder. Use this technique accompanied by a hand signal for merging left.
5. Always use hand signals. You have an obligation to let others know your intentions. Motorists can come out of nowhere and be upon you before you realize it, so don't assume there's no one to watch your signals.
6. If you think traffic is too heavy to make a left turn, continue through the intersection to the opposite corner and walk your bike across.
7. Be visible. Wear bright-colored clothing. At night you need a light and reflectors.
8. Don't carry anything in your hands. Make use of bike bags, carriers, baskets, or backpacks.
9. Be prepared for hazards including potholes, broken glass, opening of car doors, and pedestrians.
10. Always remain predictable, and behave like a vehicle.

I. As a vehicle, am I allowed on any road?

You are allowed on any road except where posted Motor Vehicles Only. When in doubt, contact the state highway department.

J. *I'd ride my bike more often, but cycling is a fair-weather sport.*

Not so! Wet-weather riding simply requires more concentration and some preparation. Industry has spent much time and energy developing components, equipment, and apparel for foul-weather riding. There are several pieces of equipment which are particularly suited to wet-weather riding, such as aluminum rims, smooth-surfaced rims, and long, soft brake pads. The bee's-nest tire pattern offers the best tire traction of all tread patterns. Snow and rain can be combated with the use of mudguards and front fender flaps. The sealing of bearings on hubs and bottom brackets, using pipe cleaners, felt, or cloth tape, will be very helpful in preventing damage to the bearings and will permit long periods of use without trouble. The chain will have to be cleaned more often. Wax the frame to maintain the finish, and clean after use.

To protect your body from the elements, parkas, pants, and chaps using Gore-Tex will keep you dry inside and out (this material has the ability to breathe). Gaiters will protect your feet and legs.

Buying a Bike

A. What speed bike should I buy?

Different types of bicycles are best suited for different uses. For riding around town, errands, and short commutes, a single-speed, 3-speed, or 5-speed is the most practical. Three-speeds require little maintenance and are easy to shift. The upright handlebars and wide saddle feel more comfortable to the beginner. For recreational riding, hilly terrain, or long-distance riding, the 10-speed is the best choice. The greater choice of ratios will allow you to enjoy longer rides.

B. Where should I buy a bike?

Buy your bike from a local reputable bicycle shop, not from an auto parts store, a department store, or a discount house. To a beginner, the $200 10-speed at the local shop looks the same as the $90 model in the discount store. It isn't. The discount bike will be heavy and use inferior components, and probably will be poorly assembled by the stock clerk. Even if the bikes were identical, the bike shop gives the following advantages:

1. You get a bike that fits you properly and fits your style of riding.
2. You get a good-quality bike that's been properly set up and adjusted.
3. You can take the bike back if anything fails and get competent repairs.
4. The bike shop's knowledgeable personnel can be an enormous help to you.

C. How much should I spend?

Nationally distributed, "bike shop"-quality, name-brand 10-speeds range in price from $150 to $500. Of course you can spend more, but the adult beginner should select either the lowest-priced model or the middle-priced model in the $200 to $250 range. Another way to decide how much to spend is to determine how much you can afford and how enthusiastic you are about cycling. You can purchase a good 3-speed model for $110 to $160.

D. What about 5-speeds?

There are quite a number of upright, rear-derailleur-only bicycles available. They don't make as much sense for commuting as a 3-speed. You can't shift when you're stopped, and you have most of the maintenance problems of a derailleur bicycle. The $10 price different between a 5-speed and a 10-speed makes the latter a more attractive proposition.

E. Which bike is the best?

There is no cut-and-dry answer to this question. The best bicycle is the one that fits you comfortably and suits your needs. Don't assume that every bicycle that you see on the road is better or worse than yours. Bicycles can't all be ranked in order. If you find a comfortable bike that is easy to maneuver and is a pleasure to ride, you have the best bike for you.

F. What is a racing bike?

A racing bike is lighter than other models. It has dropped handlebars, a skinny, hard saddle, a shorter wheelbase, steeper

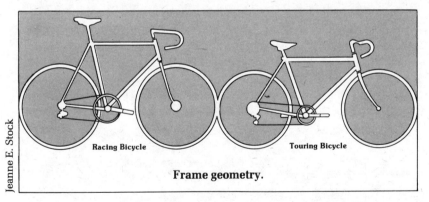

Jeanne E. Stock

Racing Bicycle   Touring Bicycle

Frame geometry.

Racing Bicycle—Short wheelbase, short chainstays, short top tube. High bottom bracket (to pedal around corners). Steep frame angles, minimum fork rake. High seat, low handlebars (minimum wind resistance). High gearing; small steps between gears.

Touring Bicycle—Long wheelbase, long chainstays, long top tube. Low bottom bracket (for minimum center of gravity). Shallow frame angles, more fork rake. Lower seat in a larger frame, higher handlebars (for more comfortable riding). Wide-range gearing; larger steps between gears.

frame angles, and a narrower gear spread. The lowest gear will be higher than a touring bicycle, and you'll have to push harder to climb hills. All bicycles with dropped handlebars are usually referred to by beginners as racing bikes. However, very few $225 bicycles are used for racing.

G. *Do I want a used bike?*

You can save some money buying a used bicycle; however, there is a trade-off. Buying a used bicycle takes more time and effort. You have to dig a little to find a prospective bicycle, and you have to inspect it when you find it. A ten-minute inspection can tell you how much it would cost you to get it fixed. Most used bicycles are in need of some repairs, and you should expect to make some to any used bicycle you buy. Only you can decide when the list of needed repairs gets too long and troublesome.

H. *Why are so many women riding men's-frame bikes?*

The top tube is absent in the traditional women's frame design. This additional tube adds strength to the men's frame design. The added frame strength helps transmit your energy to the road more efficiently. Many women enjoy hard riding and choose the men's frame for the extra strength.

I. *What is a mixte?*

A mixte is a type of bicycle frame with no top tube but with two long tubes extending from the top of the head tube to the rear fork

Sally Ann Shenk

Mixte frame.

ends instead. This construction (in comparison to the traditional women's model) distributes stress more evenly, resulting in a stronger frame.

J. *What are folding bikes? Aren't they more like a toy?*

Folding bikes are bikes with collapsible frames. They are not toys but traveler's and commuter's bikes, which can fold up quickly for convenient storage and easy carrying. Folding bikes are lightweight, ranging from approximately 18 to 25 pounds. These vehicles offer the possibility of bimodal transportation: take the bus, subway, or train partway, and bicycle the remaining distance.

The assembled, fully set-up Bickerton, with carrying bag fitted to the handlebars.

K. *I want to buy my child a new bike but don't feel he's ready to handle a 10-speed. What are my options?*

You don't have to buy your child a 10-speed. If you are considering buying a bicycle for your youngster, say anyone in the 8-to-15-year-old age range, you should consider a BMX model. Other options are 3-speeds and 10-speeds. Which you choose will depend on the needs of the child, his age, and the intended use.

L. *What is a BMX bicycle?*

A BMX bicycle is designed for children to race on a short dirt track with jumps, sharp curves, and lots of bumps. BMX bicycles come in just one frame size, and 20-inch wheels with knobby tires are standard. The frames are usually welded or hand-brazed, and

11

lugless. The $126 bicycle will have a steel frame, steel 36-spoke rims, a flat, forged fork, and steel handlebars. If you are considering a bike in the $160-plus price range, you'll find the primary improvement to be a chrome-molybdenum frame and sometimes chromemoly forks as well. These machines are single-speeds with coaster brakes. Ashtabula one-piece cranks are the accepted standard for BMX bikes, and crankarms are generally 7 to 7½ inches long. A 39-tooth front sprocket and an 18-to-20-tooth rear sprocket are fairly standard. The saddle will have a plastic or vinyl cover over a hard plastic base with a steel undercarriage. Stock machines weigh about 30 to 36 pounds. There are many options available; changes and additions can be made to fit the buyer's fancy and pocketbook.

Sally Ann Shenk and Mitch Mandel

A BMX diamond frame on the Schwinn MAG Scrambler SX 100.

M. Can I assume that the bike shop will allow me to road test a bicycle before making a purchase?

No. Road testing a bicycle is left completely to the discretion of the shop owner. However, a bike shop owner who encourages a customer to take a spin will probably win the customer's confidence and make a sale.

N. What is a typical warranty or condition of sale? What sort of service should I expect from my bicycle dealer?

Check the warranty. This is especially important for BMX bicycles. Most manufacturers offer only very limited coverage, many as little as 90 days. Quite a few don't offer any warranty. Since 3-speeds and 10-speeds aren't expected to be put to the same stress, warranties are better. When the condition of sale and warranty requires the dealer to fully assemble the bike, the frame and fork usually carry a lifetime guarantee. With suggested dealer assembly or assembly not required, you can expect a limited warranty.

The most important advice is to buy from a bicycle shop that you know and trust (or one that has been recommended to you). You'll get a quality bike that's been properly set up and adjusted. If a shop owner wants your return business, he'll give you good advice on such things as selection, size, and use. In addition, he'll carry spare parts for the brands he sells.

O. I am a heavyweight. Are there special considerations I should know about?

It might be a good idea to look for a bicycle with a lifetime warranty on the frame and fork. Also, pay special attention to your rims and spokes. Aluminum rims are lighter, but steel will give you a stronger wheel. Thicker, stronger spokes are available. The best are 14-gauge carbon steel spokes. And they're also the cheapest!

Frame

A. How do I know what size bicycle to buy?

Generally, you can closely approximate your proper frame size by taking the measurement of your inseam to the floor (in bare feet) and subtracting 10 inches. Slight adjustments may be required if you have long legs and a relatively short torso or if you have short legs and a long torso.

B. What is the best tubing?

There is no "best" tubing. Many brands of tubing are excellent; however, the most popular, top-grade tube sets are manufactured by TI Reynolds in England and A. L. Colombo in Italy.

C. What is butted tubing?

Butted tubing is a lightweight tube that maintains the same outside diameter. Its inside diameter, however, is less at one or both

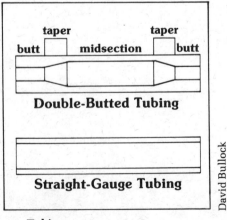

Tubing.

ends of the tube. In other words, the wall thickness of the tubing is greater at the butted end.

D. *What is straight-gauge tubing?*

Straight-gauge tubing has exactly the same wall thickness throughout the entire length of the tube.

E. *What is brazing?*

Brazing is a process by which two metal surfaces are joined by heating and melting a third substance such as brass or silver.

F. *What is the advantage of buying a custom-built frame?*

Presuming the builder is experienced and knowledgeable, a custom frame can be built that conforms to your individual physique. It can be designed to respond to your riding needs, and it can be equipped with whatever equipment or features you require.

G. *I'd like to build my own bicycle. Where can I purchase tubing?*

Reynolds tubing: Proteus Design
9225 Baltimore Boulevard
College Park, MD 20740

Columbus tubing: Ultima
P.O. Box 37426
Houston, TX 77036

H. *I have a bent frame. What can I do about it?*

Correction of a bent frame depends on the degree of damage. A severely bent tube that is kinked cannot be straightened without a significant loss of strength. If the frame is an expensive one, it might be worthwhile to have a frame builder replace the damaged tube(s). If the tube is not kinked, a good bicycle shop or frame builder should be able to straighten it without any significant loss of strength.

I. *What is meant by frame whip?*

Frame whip is the tendency of the frame to sway side-to-side under extreme pedaling pressure.

J. *Can I repaint my frame?*

Yes; however, specialized skills are required to obtain the lustre and chip resistance of a factory paint job. Additionally, much of the resale value of a top-quality frame can be lost if repainted, because it may be difficult to determine the manufacturer after a complete repainting.

K. *What are the advantages and disadvantages of chroming? Anodizing?*

A chrome frame avoids normal paint chipping, it looks spectacular when clean, and it is basically rust resistant if it is kept waxed. It is also heavier, and most builders believe the chroming process encourages rusting from inside the frame tubes.

Aluminum alloy frames are anodized to eliminate oxidation.

L. *What can you do to prevent rust inside the seat tube and down tube?*

Apply oil to a rag, and force the rag through the tubes until an oily film covers the insides of the tubes.

M. *Do bicycle frames ever wear out?*

Yes, but the "wearing-out process" is only a problem with lightweight tubing in performance-oriented bicycles. The bicycle frame can become whippy or soft. Assuming proper frame-building techniques, frames last many years without any problems.

N. *What are some undesirable characteristics to avoid in a bicycle frame?*

Poor exterior finish (excess brazing material around lugs), poor paint, misalignment, and the use of super-light tubing in nonracing applications.

Brakes

A. What are coaster brakes?

Coaster brakes are contained within the rear hub of the bicycle. They work by jamming together a row of washers on the rear axle when you backpedal. Some of the washers rotate with the hub shell; others stay still with the axle. The resulting friction slows the bike down.

The coaster brake has two advantages:
1. It is fully enclosed, so that it requires little maintenance and isn't affected by weather.
2. It is operated by the feet. Foot operation makes the coaster brake especially suitable for small children, who may not have well-developed coordination in their hands.

The coaster brake has several disadvantages:
1. It can't be used with derailleur gearing because it won't work with the derailleur's slack chain and idle rollers.
2. It can't be used on the front wheel, which slows the bike down much faster than the rear wheel.
3. It overheats if you go down a very long and steep hill because it doesn't dissipate heat as well as a rim brake.

B. What are the advantages and disadvantages of sidepull versus centerpull?

The differences are vastly overstated, and fashion has made each style more popular in its own time. Sidepull brakes transmit your hand's movement to the brake shoes through a shorter and more direct chain of brake cable and brake parts. This means the brake mechanism itself is inherently stiffer, so that it is harder to flex the brake itself by squeezing the hand lever. (In particular, the sidepull brake doesn't have the centerpull brake's transverse cable. When you actuate a centerpull brake, you use great mechanical advantage to stretch the transverse cable, and only after that is done does your effort reach the brake shoes.) However, the sidepull brake lacks the centerpull brake's mechanical advantage, and persons with weak hands may find it easier to exert greater stopping power at the rim by using a well-adjusted centerpull brake. If you like to use one or two fingers on the brake lever to execute a panic stop, centerpull brakes are for you. A competent cyclist can use either style of brake with complete confidence and safety.

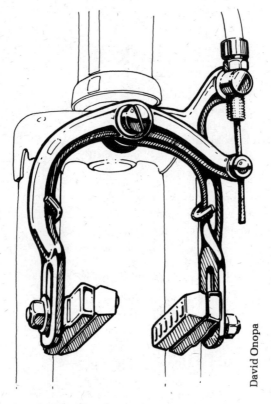

David Onopa

Sidepull brake.

C. What are cantilever brakes?

Cantilever brakes are a rarely seen item that combines the leverage of the centerpull brake with the stiffness of the sidepull brake. They are, technically, a kind of centerpull brake with the brake caliper pivots brazed onto the bicycle frame. The calipers themselves, instead of reaching across the top of the wheel like ice

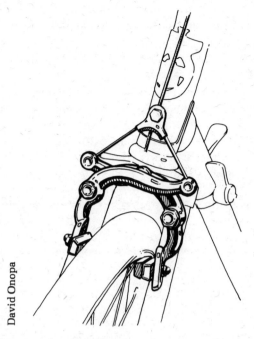

Centerpull brake.

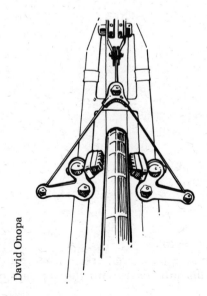

Cantilever brake.

tongs, reach out away from the center of the bike. The calipers are shorter and stiffer than those on ordinary centerpull brakes, but the extra-long transverse cable gives added mechanical advantage. Cantilever brakes are most often seen on touring bikes and tandems, where greater stopping power is needed.

D. My brakes squeal. Is something wrong?

Bicycle mechanics fix squealing brakes because the noise is annoying, not because the brakes are in any sort of dangerous condition. The source of the squeal is best explained by an analogy. Hold your arm out straight with your thumb down, and the thumbnail pointing toward you. Rest the tip of the thumb on a tabletop and drag the thumb toward you. Your thumb will tend to hobble and jump over the tabletop, making some noise. But if you turn your thumb so it points away from you, it will rest smoothly on the tabletop as you drag it toward you. Squealing brakes are like thumbs pointing toward you. To correct this, mechanics carefully bend the brake calipers so the front of the brake shoe strikes the rim a bit before the rear end of the brake shoe.

E. How do I lubricate brakes, and how often?

Brakes don't need much lubrication. An annual drop of oil on the brake caliper pivots should suffice unless you like to leave your bike out in the rain. Brake cables are another story, however. The brake cable inner wire should be pulled out of the casing and lubricated with a light grease at the slightest provocation. Normally, brake cable lubrication lasts for years—but many bikes need it, and few bikes need brake lubrication.

F. No matter how hard I squeeze my brake levers, I don't get enough braking power. What is wrong?

Maybe your cables need lubrication. See above. If that's not the problem, it's possible that the brakes need to be adjusted so the brake pads hit the rim sooner after you begin squeezing the hand lever. These are the most likely causes. Other possibilities include: brake calipers aren't free to pivot because the pivot has been overtightened and/or underlubricated; brake hand lever not free to pivot because of mechanical obstruction and/or lack of lubrication; brake pads too worn down; or poorly designed brake with insufficient stopping power.

G. What should I know about wet-weather braking?

Don't expect it to work very well. Ride slower in wet weather— you have much less friction between the brake pad and the rim, and much less friction between the tire and the road. Hence, it's harder to get the wheel to slow down and easier to get it to skid on the pavement. Apply your brakes early; they have to wipe water off the rim through a couple revolutions of the wheel before they have much stopping power. If your bike has steel rims and you're unhappy with its wet-weather stopping power, think about investing in aluminum rims. Among their many other advantages, they make wet-weather stopping much better.

H. *What are disc brakes?*

Disc brakes consist of a small metal disc, the size of a 45-revolutions-per-minute phonograph record, and a mechanism which pinches the disc much like a regular caliper brake pinches the rim.

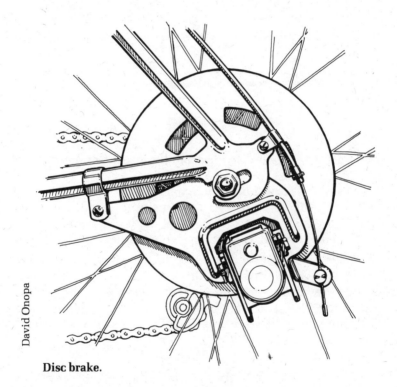

David Onopa

Disc brake.

I. *Do I need dual brake levers ("safety" levers)?*

No. They'll only teach you bad habits. Assist levers, as they're sometimes called, appeal to novice cyclists who assume that they would be forced to brake from the crouch (racing) position if they didn't have them. That's not true; good cyclists usually ride with their hands resting on the brake lever housing and apply the brakes simply by squeezing the fingers casually wrapped around the brake lever.

There's an important reason why this is a much better habit than using assist levers. Should you need to maneuver suddenly or execute a panic stop, you do want to shift to the crouch position. In that position, your center of gravity is lowered, your hands are in a position where you can maneuver the bike more precisely, and your arms and legs can act as a suspension if you need to move your weight around. If your hands are already on the brake lever housing, you can switch to the crouch position. If your hands are up on the tops, clutching the levers won't make the necessary change. Your maneuverability, and hence your safety, will be badly compromised.

Saddle

A. Why do I want a hard leather saddle instead of a soft, wide, spring model?

The leather saddle does not reduce the effectiveness of the rider's pedal stroke as much as the "mattress" saddle. The soft, springy, mattress saddle absorbs some of the leg power that should be transmitted to the pedals. Also, the wide saddle tends to chafe the tender insides of riders' thighs.

B. How do I break in a leather saddle?

A good leather saddle is properly broken in by riding, riding, and more riding. You should also apply saddle soap regularly, and if you frequently ride in the rain you should apply neat's-foot oil to the underside of the saddle.

C. Is there a cure for saddle sores?

Yes, stop riding until they heal. They usually occur from ingrown hairs which can be the result of too much riding with bicycle shorts that need cleaning. The chamois in the bicycle shorts should be kept absolutely clean.

D. How can I prevent chafing?

Assuming you are using a good saddle that is adjusted properly, proper selection of your riding clothes can eliminate chafing problems. Do not ride with short shorts that leave your flesh uncovered against the saddle. You should also avoid riding with pants like denim jeans because of the large seams in the crotch area.

E. *I've heard a lot about saddles for women. Why do women require a special saddle design?*

The pelvic structure of a woman is wider than that of a man, and the different genital structure requires different positioning.

F. *What should I know about saddle height and handlebar adjustment?*

For most riders the handlebars should be from 1 to 2 inches below the height of the saddle.

G. *How do I determine correct saddle height?*

Correct saddle height is determined by placing both heels on the pedals and raising the saddle until there is a slight bend in the knees at the bottom of the stroke. A good check is to pedal backward with both heels on the pedals; if the rider's pelvis rocks back and forth, the saddle is too high.

H. *What should I know about seat-angle adjustment for a more comfortable ride?*

The top of the saddle should be level with, or slightly higher than, the back of the saddle. This reduces pressure on the hands caused by sliding forward on the saddle.

I. *How do you care for a leather saddle?*

Regular saddle soaping takes care of most leather saddle problems. If a saddle becomes soaked in a rainstorm, it should be allowed to dry naturally. Do not place it near a heater or fire. After it has dried, saddle soap should be applied.

J. *What are the advantages of plastic- or leather-covered plastic saddles over all-leather saddles?*

Plastic-base saddles do not require breaking in, since they do not change. They are impervious to cold, heat, or water. They are also lighter.

Handlebars

A. What are randonneur handlebars?

Randonneur handlebars are dropped handlebars with tops that rise slightly from the center before bending forward; the lower grips bend out slightly. They are specifically designed for touring, but many tourists prefer the more common style of dropped handlebars called maes.

B. Do I have to have dropped handlebars?

No, but when you know all the reasons why other people have them, you'll probably at least want to try them. Ordinary handlebars restrict you to keeping your hands in one position. With dropped handlebars, there are several positions, and you can shift among them so you don't get tired of any one position.

In all of the hand positions, your hands are further away from your body than they are with upright handlebars. That's an important asset, because it allows you to stretch out your arms and keep from feeling cramped.

Dropped handlebars shift some of your weight off the saddle and onto the handlebars. This reduces the wear and tear on your derriere, and it changes the bike's center of gravity to allow you to handle the bike better, especially in situations requiring quick maneuvering.

Now perform a little test to convince yourself how much more efficiently your leg muscles work when you have dropped handlebars on your bike. Sit up straight. Without bending over, try to stand up. Pretty hard, isn't it? Now bend over and try it. See? Your muscles work less hard when you're in the bent-over position.

There's more. Your spine is stretched as much as 3 inches longer than it would be in an upright position. That's good for it, and relaxing for you.

C. *Where should I place my hands on the handlebars when I ride?*

First, realize that you don't pedal very much with your hands on the "drops" (the lower section of dropped handlebars). Most of the time you'll move your hands between several different positions on the top of the handlebars. You use the dropped position for an extra power spurt or for a change of pace.

D. *Numb hands are a real problem for me. What can I do?*

The problem of numb hands is usually due to the nerves between bones in the wrist compressing against the handlebars. There are several solutions to the problem, including padding by means of gloves or on the handlebars. If the problem continues, it is probably necessary to go to a more upright riding position using a shorter handlebar stem, or, if that fails, flat bars. This puts more weight on the rear end, and a change of saddle may be necessary. A shorter stem will decrease the angle of your body, thus reducing the amount of weight leaning on the bars. Change hand position frequently, shifting weight onto the fleshy area of the palm just behind the thumb.

E. *Are dropped bars better than upright handlebars for touring?*

The dropped-style handlebar is used by most experienced cyclists whether for racing, touring, or commuting. It allows for better weight distribution; a lowered center of gravity; and a choice of hand positions which includes the bottom of the drops, resting on the brake levers, or the top of the bars.

F. *What are the effects of a handlebar stem that is too long or too short?*

If the stem is too short the shoulder muscles will hurt. Those muscles are the most unnecessarily overworked muscles a bicycle rider has. They support and hold the spine in a position to work and transmit that work to the legs. If the stem is too long, the arm and neck muscles will hurt.

Stem

A. Why is stem length so important in terms of comfortable riding?

The stem length determines the point of support for your upper body. If the stem is too long, the rider will develop sore hands, arms, and back and neck muscles. If the stem is too short, the rider may develop back problems, and the rider's ability to breathe will be impaired, especially when using the drops of the handlebars.

B. How do I check for proper stem length?

You should check the position of your upper body in each of the three basic handlebar positions to determine which stem length is appropriate:

Handlebar position #1:
> (Hands on top of handlebars, center.) The rider's back should be above 45 degrees.

Handlebar position #2:
> (Hands on top of handlebars, behind brake levers.) The rider's back should have a smooth bend and be at, or slightly below, 45 degrees.

Handlebar position #3:
> (Hands on the drops of the handlebars.) The rider's back should have a smooth bend and be below 45 degrees. A plumb line dropped from the rider's nose should fall approximately 1 inch behind the handlebar.

C. What is the value of adjustable stems?

An adjustable stem permits easy, convenient adjustments to determine proper handlebar extension. They are expensive and heavy, and some may slip in use.

D. *Why are some stems super-expensive? What separates these from the cheaper stems?*

The basic differences between expensive and inexpensive stems are the degree of final finishing and, most important, the strength-to-weight ratio. The best stems are lighter than inexpensive stems, but they are as strong or stronger. This strength-to-weight ratio requires costly alloy and manufacturing processes.

Headset

A. What is a headset?

The headset consists of the bearing mechanism which allows the bicycle's steering to pivot. The two sets of headset bearings are located one at each end of the frame's head tube; bearing cups are the little silver rings pressed into each end of the head tube, and the bearing cones are located on the fork's steering tube.

B. How can I tell if my headset is loose?

Pick up the bike and try to rattle the front fork. If you can feel any play in it, that's a sure sign. When you're riding and you apply the front-wheel brake, a loose headset will cause the bike to buck slightly.

C. What effect will a loose headset have on my riding and safety?

The bucking feeling it gives you (see above) can make the bike harder to control. It can be harder to keep the bike pointed where you want it to go, especially over rough pavement.

D. How can I avoid headset damage?

If you keep the headset at the proper level of tightness, it won't have a chance to rattle around and cause itself wear and tear.

E. What maintenance is required?

The headset's lower bearing picks up a lot of road grit, and this grit eventually works its way into the bearing surfaces. Accordingly, you should disassemble, clean, and regrease your headset periodically. How often depends on (a) how well protected you headset is against dirt, and (b) how much you ride in the rain. As a rough guide, most mechanics recommend an annual overhaul.

Forks

A. What is fork rake?

Fork blades are bent slightly forward to improve the bicycle's handling characteristics and ride comfort. This bend is called fork rake.

B. If my fork is bent, can I bend it back into place?

If you have to ask, the answer is no. Bending a fork back can be done, but there are many little tricks you need to know to do it properly. You only get one chance to try, so if you try and botch the job, the fork can't be fixed. And many bicycle mechanics prefer to use specialized—and expensive—tools for fork bending.

C. How can I tell if my fork is bent?

Lean the bicycle against a wall, and walk away from it so you can look at it from the side. Look closely at the fork. It should not curve backward from the fork crown. It should extend straight down from the fork crown and then begin to curve forward. If it curves backward, it's bent. This kind of fork damage is the most common, and also the hardest to detect. Other fork damage is likely to be asymmetrical, bending one fork blade sideways. You can easily detect such damage by visual inspection.

D. What is a dropout?

A dropout is the small piece of metal brazed into the bottom tip of the fork. Its purpose is to provide a slot for the wheel to clamp into, and also eyelets where fender and carrier braces may be attached. A similar piece of metal which the rear wheel clamps into is also called the dropout.

E. *Why are dropouts designed in so many different ways?*

Dropouts vary according to the function of the bike. Dropouts for racing bikes do not have fender eyelets.

Rear-wheel dropouts vary in other ways. The better ones have a special fitting on the right dropout; the derailleur clamps right into this fitting, eliminating the need for a separate derailleur hanger. They also generally have set screws to help you position the wheel into a horizontal slot, with an opening toward the front of the bike, some use a vertical slot. Track bike dropouts have a horizontal slot with the opening toward the rear.

Front-wheel dropouts are almost all quite similar. One exception is a patented dropout made by Ross. This dropout requires you to fish the axle around a corner when you remove the wheel. This feature greatly reduces the danger of an accident from the wheel suddenly falling off the bicycle.

Tires

A. What are tire savers?

Also referred to as thorn catchers and flint catchers, these are small wires held near the brakes so that they drag lightly across the surface of the tire tread to expel damaging debris from the tire.

B. I am plagued with flat tires. What are my alternatives?

Have you tried tire savers? Are you careful to avoid glass and potholes? Get thicker tires and thorn-proof (extra-thick) inner tubes. If you are still having trouble, there are several manufacturers of punctureless tires. The Never-Air is an airless tube made of plastic material that can be fitted inside an ordinary tire. The material is reasonably resilient. Although it is heavier than regular tubes, it is relatively easy to ride on once speed is reached. Another company offers a urethane composition tube filler. Injected through the air valve to the same pressure as the tire's rated air pressure, the liquid cures overnight, becoming solid but resilient. The additional weight will be several pounds.

C. Why do bicycle tires require a higher pressure than automobile tires?

For ride comfort, automobile tires are designed to absorb more road shock than you would want bicycle tires to. A bicycle feels awful with automobile-level tire pressures. It's sluggish and unresponsive. Moreover, the increased rolling resistance makes the bike much harder to pedal.

D. *What pressure should I pump my tires to? Is it important to keep them inflated to a certain pressure?*

Manufacturers' tire pressure recommendations should be followed except in special circumstances. Heavy riders should increase their tire pressures by 10 to 15 pounds per square inch, while lighter riders can get away with lower pressures than the recommended ones. Since most of a rider's weight is over the rear wheel, the front tire can usually be run at 10 to 15 pounds per square inch lower than the rear. Some cyclists lower their tire pressures to allow for expansion on hot days, but this is unnecessary. If, however, you plan to zip down mountain passes all day, lowering pressures is a good idea. Long, hard braking can raise the pressure of your tires.

Many cyclists like to use as much tire pressure as they can get away with. The limiting factor is quite simple: too much pressure will unseat the tire, and it will peel off the rim and blow out. You should inspect the entire circumference of the tire on both sides whenever you add air.

E. *Do tubulars require any special care?*

Yes. Take the usual precautions, such as using tire savers and latex proofing solution, and check for glass. You should deflate tubulars when not in use to relax their casing threads so the tires retain their strength and elasticity. Store the bike with its weight off the wheels; this is a good idea for any bike you plan to store for a long time.

F. *Can I use a gas station air hose to inflate my tires?*

Use gas station air hoses only in emergencies. Air rushing in as rapidly as these pumps allow can stretch a tube excessively in one spot before filling the rest of it. If you must use such a hose, use it in short bursts, checking your tires with an accurate pressure gauge after each burst and making sure the tire is seating evenly.

G. *What one step will make the biggest difference in lightening my bike?*

The easiest way to upgrade the ride and performance of any bicycle is by giving it a better set of wheels. Shedding a pound and a half from a bike's wheels can drastically affect performance. Since the tires, tubes, and rims rotate much faster than any other components, their weight is twice as important as that of components which don't rotate.

H. *What are Schrader and Presta valves?*

Schrader valves are tire valves similar to auto tire valves. Presta valves are smaller valves used only on bicycle tires. They use a thumbscrew instead of a spring to hold the valve shut. They're found on tubulars and on lightweight tires. They require a special hand pump or an adapter to use with an air hose.

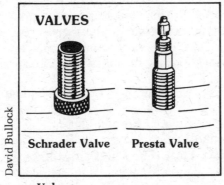

Valves.

I. What is rolling resistance?

There are a number of factors which contribute to rolling resistance, including total weight, hub-bearing friction, area of tire contact with ground, and tire sidewall flex. The largest contributor to rolling resistance is internal friction. For instance, the flattening out of the tire as it contacts the ground (and its return to the original shape after rotating through the bottom of the revolution) takes energy away from the wheel. Wind resistance, however, saps more of your energy than rolling resistance.

J. What are the two types of tires, and what are the advantages and disadvantages of each?

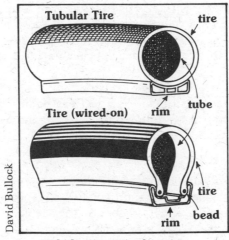

Tubular tire. Wired-on tire.

The first type of bicycle tire, which is standard on most bicycles, is the wired-on tire, sometimes referred to as a clincher. This tire contains a bead which catches in a lip on the rim, sandwiching a separate tube in between. The tubular, or sew-up tire, in comparison, is sewn closed around its tube and is glued to the rim. Advantages of wired-on tires are durability, ease of repair, and low cost. Advantages of tubular tires are speed, responsiveness, and ease of riding.

K. *Why do they make bicycle tires so skinny? What happened to the old balloon tires?*

The old balloon tires are heavy and spongy so that you waste a lot of time turning them. High-pressure tires, on the other hand, will give a solid and fast ride. Balloon tires are still available and could be right for the kind of riding you do. No tire is perfect. Each compromises lightness for durability, rolling resistance for shock absorption, strength for price.

L. *The gumwall of my tires is cracking. Does this mean I need new tires?*

Gumwall cracks are superficial as a rule. Ozone caused by auto air pollution and sunlight cause them. You can ride on these tires, but if the cracks are too deep and the threads aren't nylon, water will get in and rot the threads. Most keen riders buy new tires every year.

M. *What is meant by "cured" tires?*

Aging, curing, or seasoning a tubular is accomplished by storing tubulars away for at least six months in a cool, dark, dry place before using. This procedure makes the tubular more durable and somewhat more puncture resistant. The fibers and cords of the tubular are strengthened. Experienced riders always have a stock of six to ten tubulars laid away. New tubulars are soft and cut easily. Don't try to age them off a rim. The tubular could take a twist, making future mounting difficult.

Another curing theory for consideration is to mount a new tubular, ride it for 50 to 100 miles, then (leaving it on the rim) put it away to cure for use the following year or later. In this way the curing will occur on a preconditioned tubular and result in a more uniform depth of cure.

N. *What are the advantages of silk tubulars?*

Silk is the strongest material (weight for weight), lasts longest, holds its shape well, and is the most expensive. For touring or racing, silks are more responsive and last longer, easily justifying the high cost. Silk is not as susceptible to water damage as cotton is.

O. Can you explain the size markings that appear on the walls of tires?

Measurement markings appear on the drilled faces of bicycle rims as well as on the walls of the tires. For example, 26 × 1¼ means the overall tread-to-tread measurement of the inflated tire fitted to the correct rim is 26 inches, and the width of the tire is 1¼ inches. So a rim marked 26 isn't really 26 inches in diameter; it's designed for a 26-inch tire. When a tire has three markings (such as 26 × 1½ × 1⅝), the middle figure refers to the rim size. The last is the actual width of the tire. The example above should be an oversize tire made with beads to fit a 1½-inch rim.

P. What is rim tape?

Rim tape is tape—or, in most cases, a thin rubber strip—which protects the inner tube from the sharp edges of the spoke nipples. It's often called rim strip.

Users of tubular tires sometimes use a special double-sided adhesive cloth rim tape to glue the tire to the rim. Glue from a tube is more popular than rim tape for this purpose.

Q. What is vulcanization? What is cold-processing?

Tire treads are attached to the casings in one of two ways. In vulcanization, a strip of rubber compound, molded to a tread pattern, is partially melted into the casing cords. Tires and inexpensive tubulars are vulcanized, but the best tubulars are cold-processed.

In cold-processing, the manufacturer attaches the tread strip by hand to the casing, gluing it in place with latex solution. The process is more expensive and time-consuming than vulcanization but does not use heat which softens treads and makes sidewalls brittle. Additionally, the treads of cold-processed tires, being positioned by hand, are straighter and track better.

R. My problem is that I get holes in my inner tube right next to the valve stem. Holes in this position can't be patched. What can I do to prevent this?

Make a leather washer of approximately ⅛-inch thickness, and slip this over the valve inside the rim.

S. After patching my tire, upon inflation, the patch gives out. What am I doing wrong?

You may be pressing on the patch too soon. Let the cement dry a bit longer. You might also be inflating too quickly after patching, or inflating before putting the tube into the tire and rim. Tubes should be inflated just enough to take shape for this step.

T. *What are some clues to underinflation?*

Underinflated tires are harder to push. The low pressures allow a large tire patch to hit the road, creating higher rolling resistance. If the pressure is extremely low, hitting a bump or stone could puncture the tube or dent the rim. You may also notice cracks in the sidewalls due to excess pliancy.

U. *What causes blowouts?*

Overinflation can cause the tire to blow right off the rim. To avoid this, use your own tire pressure gauge and check the pressure frequently while filling. Be aware that air pressure in tires will increase due to rim heating from brake friction and from hot weather.

V. *My tire threads wear unevenly. Why?*

Uneven wear can be due to tire misalignment, an out-of-round rim, skidding the tires when braking, and grabby brakes.

W. *Are there special tires for riding in wet weather?*

Tire thread pattern plays an important role in wet-weather

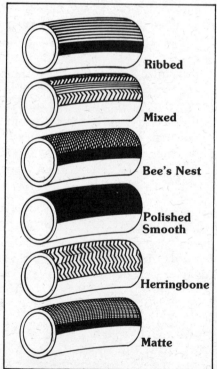

Ribbed

Mixed

Bee's Nest

Polished Smooth

Herringbone

David Bullock

Matte

Tread patterns.

riding. Most tires have a ribbed pattern in the center, with her-ringbone sidewalls for good gripping on wet roads and around turns. An all-herringbone pattern has better traction on the straights, but the bee's-nest pattern has the best traction of all in wet or dry weather. Matte and smooth treads are slippery when wet.

Rims and Spokes

A. What is meant by truing a wheel? What is a truing jig?

"Truing" a wheel involves tightening or loosening each spoke to make the rim a perfect circle or, in other terms, to make it run "true." A truing jig is a fixture that holds the wheel in place during the truing process. The jig can be as simple as the front fork of a bicycle, or a complex device that includes dial indicators that measure the "wobble" of the rim in thousands of an inch!

B. How do alloy rims compare with steel rims in terms of weight and strength?

In general, alloy rims are lighter than steel rims. They have different characteristics, however. Steel rims are malleable, and dents can be bent back to approximate their predented shape. Alloy rims will "bounce back" into their original shape when hitting small bumps, but a big bump or chuckhole may dent the rim sufficiently that it requires replacement. Alloy rims cannot be bent and rebent like steel rims.

C. What is meant by dishing?

A bicycle wheel is built so that the rim is centered on the axle. Now, when you build a front wheel, the rim will be centered on the axle without any special effort on your part. But when you build a rear wheel, you must "dish" the wheel to center it on the axle.

Dishing involves tightening all spoke nipples on the freewheel side of the wheel an extra three or four turns. Why? On the rear wheel, the hub flanges aren't centered on the axle. The freewheel-side (right) hub flange is mounted further in, toward the center of the hub, to make room for the freewheel. So the rim must be closer to that flange than it is to the nonfreewheel-side (left) hub flange.

Ray Wolf

The wheel in the truing stand, ready for both truing and rounding.

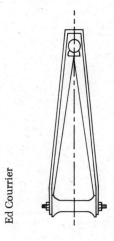 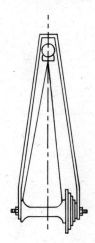

Ed Courrier

Dishing.

D. *What is radial spoking? Tangent? Are there other spoking patterns? Which is most common, and what are the advantages?*

A radial-spoked wheel has its spokes meeting the rim at right angles. No spokes cross each other. Tangent spoking occurs with all other wheel lacing patterns, 2X, 3X, 4X (two-cross, three-cross, four-cross), since the spokes enter the rim at a tangent, or angle.

The 3X and 4X patterns are most common, since they provide optimum balance of strength, shock absorption, stability, and reliability.

E. *How do I decide what type of rims and spokes I should have?*

Use the advice of a competent wheel builder. You should match the intended use of the wheel with the components to be selected. The wheel builder will be able to recommend hub, rim, and spoke combinations to match the technical building requirements and your riding needs.

F. *How do you determine your own wheel spoking?*

Follow the path of any single spoke in the wheel—how many spokes cross over, or under, it? That number is referred to as 2X, 3X, or 4X.

G. *How do you determine spoke length?*

If you have a complete wheel and require a spoke, determine the proper size by matching the replacement spoke side-by-side with a spoke in the wheel.

Tangent spoking.

Sally Ann Shenk

H. What is spoke gauge? How do you determine a suitable spoke gauge?

The spoke gauge is the thickness or diameter of the spoke. You must match the spoke gauge to your riding needs (tandems require heavier spokes than singles, for instance) and the hubs that you have. Consult your local bicycle shop for advice.

I. What are the advantages of short and long spoke nipples?

Short spoke nipples may provide more threads to hold the spoke.

J. What is meant by wheel stiffness?

Wheel stiffness is a general term that is often misused to include different characteristics. It can refer to the characteristics of the specific spoking pattern. For instance, a radial-spoked wheel transmits the impact of a bump directly to the rider. It does not absorb the bump. Some riders refer to that as a stiff wheel. The term can also refer to the amount of spoke tension and the responsiveness of the wheel. Racers generally describe a component as stiff if it does not absorb power from their pedal stroke.

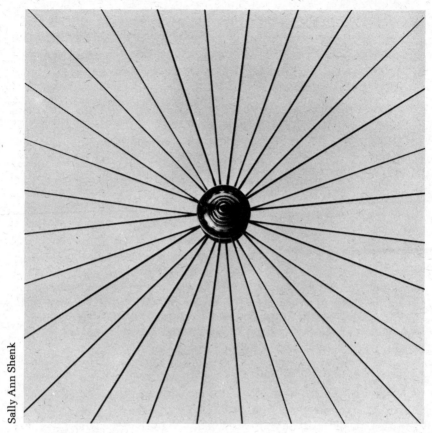

Sally Ann Shenk

Radial spoking.

K. What causes spokes to break?

Spokes break for obvious reasons like rusting or crashing. Other than that, they break because of unequal spoke tension in the wheel. This unequal tension can increase the load on one or two spokes beyond the breaking point. Spokes in the rear wheel tend to break because they have the job of transmitting torque from the hub to the rim, and this puts them under constant stress.

L. Why are most wheels laced (spoked) with 36 spokes but some with 24, 28, 32, 40, or other amounts?

Thirty-six-spoke wheels meet the needs of most cyclists. Heavy racers or tandem riders frequently need the increased strength gained by 40-spoke wheels. To them, the increased reliability is worth the marginal increase in weight. Twenty-four-, 28- and 32 spoke wheels should be used only in races where weight is more important than strength. Twenty-four- and 28-spoke wheels are usually used only in record attempts or time trials where stress is less than in mass-start races.

M. *Will my wheel collapse when I replace a single spoke?*
No.

N. *What is the best way to fix a flat and change a tire and tube on the back wheel of a derailleur bicycle?*
Presuming you are fixing a flat on a wired-on tire, the easiest method is to remove the rear wheel. To remove the rear wheel, first shift the rear derailleur and chain onto smallest (high gear) freewheel cog. This places the derailleur in its most "outside" position. Loosen the quick release, or axle nuts, and push the wheel forward. The freewheel will probably contact the top derailleur pulley and not fall free. Grab the derailleur body and pull it back. It is spring-loaded and should move freely. The wheel should now fall free.

Once you have repaired the flat, installation of the wheel is not difficult. Remember to start the chain on the small cog, or the derailleur will be out of line and the wheel will be hard to position. The installation procedure is simply the removal procedure in reverse.

O. *Can I repair a broken spoke?*
No.

P. *How do I avoid wheel wobble?*
The spokes must be properly tensioned to keep the wheel true.

Hubs

A. What is the difference between small-flange and large-flange hubs?

Hubs are available with low (small) flanges, high (large) flanges, and medium flanges. There is no set standard to determine when one is low-flange and one high. However, it is normally recognized that if the hub flange diameter is between 30 and 45 millimeters, it's considered to be a low flange; between 45 and 60 millimeters, a medium flange; and 60 millimeters and up is a high flange.

The width of the flange relates to the wheel use and riding characteristics desired. A low flange will require a longer spoke, giving the wheel more flex and resiliency. Small-flange hubs are for serious road racing and touring where vibrations must be cut to a minimum and when comfort is desirable. Large-flange hubs are used for track riding for sheer rigidity and responsiveness. They're often found on road bicycles that have very flexible frames. The large flange enables the rider to accelerate and decelerate quickly, with a minimum of energy-consuming wheel flex. There is also a faster reaction to transmission of power in the explosive sprints seen in this type of riding. Very stiff wheels, if used on the road, will loosen your head bearings, make your wrists ache, give your legs lots of unwanted vibration, and cause spoke breakages, because they are too stiff to absorb road shocks from bumps and holes. The medium-flange hubs are for track, hill climbing, small circuits, and races.

B. What are the advantages of sealed-bearing hubs?

For many years the only type of hub available had loose ball bearings and adjustable cones. Maintenance involved disassembly, cleaning, and repacking the bearings. With sealed bearings, the units

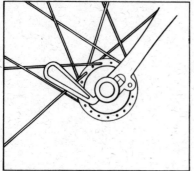

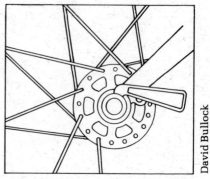

David Bullock

Low-flange hub. Four-cross pattern.   **High-flange hub. Three-cross pattern.**

come already assembled, lubricated, and adjusted. Maintenance involves returning the entire unit to the factory.

C. *What are quick-release hubs?*

Quick-release hubs do not require the use of a wrench to remove the wheel. They are kept in the bike by a locking cam and released by a lever.

David Onopa

Quick-release hub.

Pedals

A. There are a lot of different kinds of pedals. Which is best?

Rubber pedals are okay for casual riding, especially when you're not going very far or you're wearing shoes not well suited to cycling.

There are several styles of all-metal pedals. The cheapest will not accept toe clips, and they're cheaply constructed. Many cannot be serviced.

Many cheap metal pedals will accept toe clips and can be serviced; among these, there are some things to look for. The pedal should be very narrow; barely wide enough to accommodate your shoe. Extra width only allows your foot to move around, and you don't want that; you want your foot to stay in precisely the correct position. Unfortunately, most cheap pedals are too wide.

Another bad style you'll often see is the counterweighted pedal. This pedal is intended to be stepped on on one side only. Reflectors extend far down on the bottom side. The one-side-only feature isn't inherently bad—all the most expensive pedals are made that way—but when you step on the wrong side of counterweighted pedals, you bend the soft metal and damage the pedal. The counterweight feature is supposed to keep the right side up for you at all times, but it doesn't always work, and it never works when you add toe clips.

The favorite style of most serious cyclists is the quill pedal. Quill pedals have a one-piece bail (or cage) which wraps around the outside of your foot. This wraparound feature makes the pedal like a cradle. When used in combination with toe clips, quill pedals provide a well-shaped cavity for your foot to slide into. The advantage is that you don't have to expend much effort to keep your foot in the proper position.

B. *Should I use toe clips?*

If you feel at all uncomfortable or unsteady on the bike, then no. But after you've been riding a while and feel accustomed to your bike, you should try them. They'll take some getting used to, but once you're used to them, you won't dream of giving them up.

Toe clips help you keep your foot in the proper position on the pedal; they allow you to spread out the effort of pedaling among more muscles; and they allow you to pull up on the pedals as well as push down, giving you added power when you want it. You'll probably find that toe clips increase your natural pedaling cadence by about 30% with no added effort on your part.

C. *Which pedals work best with toe clips?*

Quill pedals. See answer to A.

D. *Which pedals will accommodate cleats?*

Any all-metal pedal will accommodate cleats. Again, quill pedals are a nearly universal favorite.

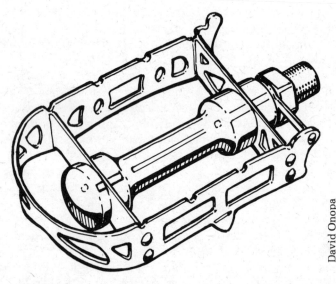

David Onopa

Quill pedal.

Pedaling Technique

A. What is pedal cadence?

In order to ride well you have to establish a steady rate of pedaling. This is known as maintaining the proper pedal cadence. For most cyclists, a good rate or cadence is 60 to 85 revolutions per minute. There is no absolutely right cadence. You have to try and find a rate best suited to your ability.

B. What cadence do racers run at?

It depends on the event. You won't see them spinning less than 90 and often they'll spin 120 to 130 revolutions per minute and up.

C. Should I stand up when pedaling?

Getting out of the saddle is a technique used in hill climbing. It allows the rider to change position and aids circulation. However, an experienced rider does not stand all the way up a hill. He should be able to take the climb sitting down.

D. Will I get more exercise if I'm pedaling hard?

Many new cyclists make the mistake of selecting a high gear and trying to exercise themselves by pushing at it as hard as they can. Although this makes you feel tired, it isn't very good exercise, and it's not the easiest or fastest way to ride. Select a gear low enough so that you can barely feel any effort to spin the pedals. Spin the pedals at a smooth clip, with the pedal revolutions per minute between 60 and 85. If this cadence makes you feel uncomfortable, slow down and work up to this level gradually. Pedaling should always feel smooth and easy.

Cranks

A. *What are the three types of cranks?*
   The three types of cranks are Ashtabula, cottered, and cotterless.

B. *Why should I want to change from a cottered crank to a cotterless crank?*

Cottered crankarm.

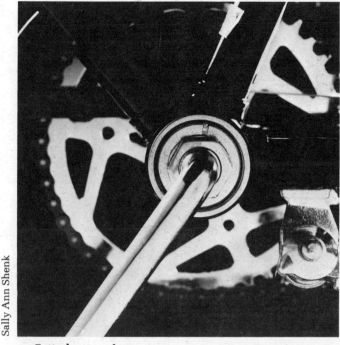

Sally Ann Shenk

Cotterless crankarm.

Cotterless cranks are usually made of lightweight alloy and are lighter. Additionally, the cotterless method of crankarm attachment is superior in principle to the cottered method.

C. *What is meant by Ashtabula?*

The Ashtabula crank is a one-piece unit which combines both crankarms and the bottom bracket axle.

It has become the standard crank in inexpensive middleweight and heavyweight bicycles. The name is derived from the place of manufacture, Ashtabula, Ashtabula County, Ohio, and from the manufacturer, ABS Industries. The company recently changed its name from the Ashtabula Bow-Socket Company.

D. *What factors influence the decision about crankarm length?*

Most cyclists should not concern themselves over the length of crankarms—the 170-millimeter size normally supplied is fine. Serious racers who have the benefit of advice from trained coaches may select alternative sizes—riders with short legs may go to 168- or 165-millimeter crankarms; riders with long legs (or time trialists and climbers) may go to 172- or 175-millimeter crankarms.

49

Ashtabula.

Tom Gettings

E. Many of my friends have switched from the standard 170-milli-meter crankarm that came with their bicycles to 180-millimeter crankarms, claiming that the extra leverage makes hills effortless and higher gears possible on the flats. Is this true?

In general terms, presuming the cyclist knows how to pedal properly, performance increases may be realized with longer crank-arms. This presumes optimum cycling strokes and training.

F. There is an annoying clicking noise when I bring the pedal around. What is causing this?

The clicking noise can be the result of any one of the following:

1. Bottom bracket bearing problems—a broken bearing or dirt in the cups.
2. The front derailleur cage is hitting against the right crankarm.
3. A broken bearing or dirt in the bearing in the pedal axle.
4. Something may be loose. The most likely (and hard-to-detect) culprit is the bottom bracket lock ring. Bearings in the pedals or crank axle may be too loose, or pedals might not be screwed tightly into the crankarms.

G. Neglect of a cotterless crank can lead to very expensive repairs. What preventive maintenance keeps me from having to make these repairs?

Always check to insure that the crank-fixing bolts are tight. If they loosen while riding, the bottom bracket axle can "chew up" the soft alloy crankarm. The other critical item is the process of screwing pedals into the crankarms. Always apply a light coating of grease to the threads to prevent damage to the soft crankarm threads.

Bottom Brackets

A. What do I need to know about the bottom bracket assembly?

The bottom bracket takes more stress than any other part of the bicycle frame. When you push on the pedals, you exert a powerful sideways force on the bottom bracket; a bicycle frame must be strong and stiff to withstand this sideways force.

The crank axle runs through the center of the bottom bracket, and its two ball bearing assemblies sit one on either side of the bottom bracket. These ball bearings need periodic adjustment, cleaning, and regreasing.

Chain

A. Why do I need a special riveting tool to take off my chain? My old bike had a master link.

The master link on your old bike is too wide to fit through the derailleur pulleys or onto the rear freewheel of a 10-speed bike. So, for years, manufacturers simply have not had master links. Now, a few manufacturers are beginning to market specially designed, extra-narrow master links.

B. When is it necessary to replace a chain?

A chain sustains wear at the point at which the link pins run through the rollers. That's where all the friction occurs, and it makes the holes in the rollers grow larger than they're supposed to be.

Eventually, the chain grows longer than it was, and it develops excess lateral flexibility. When this happens, the chain doesn't shift as well, and it grates on the cog and chainwheel teeth, causing added wear.

A chain can take years to wear out, or it can happen in a week if you leave your bike out in the rain.

To tell if your chain is worn out, measure 24 links. The links are supposed to be ½ inch each, and 24 links should measure 12 inches. When they reach 12 ⅛ inches, it's time to replace the chain.

C. *Why does my chain come off the sprockets?*

There are many, many reasons why this happens. The only thing you can say for sure is that it's virtually never the fault of the chain.

Before considering the possible causes, let's talk about sprockets. That's an imprecise word. The sprockets connected to the rear crankset are called chainwheels. The sprockets connected to the rear wheel are called cogs. Most cyclists have more trouble with the chain coming off the chainwheels than with the chain coming off the cogs.

If the chain comes off the cogs, by jamming between the smallest cog and the frame or by jamming between the largest cog and the rear wheel spokes, your rear derailleur is undoubtedly out of adjustment.

If the chain comes off the chainwheels, consider the following possible problems:

1. Is your shifting technique okay? Do you move the derailleur to disengage the chain from the small chainwheel, and then begin spinning the pedals like mad? If you do that, the chain will skate along the top of the large chainwheel teeth, rather than meshing with them.
2. Is your front derailleur properly adjusted? It should have just enough range of motion to stay clear of the chain when you shift into the two extreme gears (small cog-large chainwheel and large cog-small chainwheel). If it can travel any further than it has to to meet these conditions, it can throw the chain off.
3. Do you have correct chainline alignment? The middle cog on your freewheel should align with the space between the two chainwheels. If it doesn't, the frame may be misaligned, the rear wheel may need a spacer washer in a particular place, or the chainwheels may be in improper position. The latter can be due to incorrect crank axle length, crank axle installed backward at the factory, or bent chainwheel spider.

4. What about the tooth shape on your chainwheels?
Chainwheel teeth have to be shaped "just so" for a derailleur
shifting mechanism to work properly. On some bikes,
especially cheaper, older bikes, chainwheel teeth tended to be
too blunt in shape. The chain tends to "walk" up and off dull
chainwheel teeth.

D. What maintenance is needed?

The chain must be kept lubricated, and it ought to be kept clean
and reasonably free of road muck. Without enough lubrication, the
chain will wear quickly and die an early death. Too much
lubrication—i.e., a chain dripping with oil—attracts excess road
muck, so you should steer a middle course.

Lubricate the chain by placing a drop of light machine oil on
each link. Spin the pedals so the chain is exercised and the oil is
worked into the working surfaces inside each chain link. That's
where the oil is needed. Now grab a rag and wipe excess oil off the
outside of the chain. Oil the chain if the bike gets wet.

To clean off road muck, give the chain a kerosene bath, then
relubricate it.

Chainwheels

A. What are chainwheels made of? How do I check chainwheel wear?

Chainwheels are made of aluminum alloy or steel. The best way to check chainwheel wear is to examine the tooth shape closely. The leading and trailing edge of the tooth should be symmetrical.

B. What is a triple chainwheel?

A triple chainwheel is three chainwheels up front which will give you 15 speeds with a 5-speed cluster and 18 speeds with a 6-speed cluster.

C. Do I need a triple chainwheel?

Fifteen speeds are useful in hill terrain and for mountain touring.

D. Could you explain the terms gear-cut *and* stamped-out *in reference to chainrings?*

Gear-cut chainrings are machined individually, so that the tooth shape differs somewhat on differing sizes of chainrings.

Stamped-out or mass-produced rings will have the same-shaped tooth on all sizes of rings. Making special shapes for differing sizes will cost more.

E. What is an elliptical chainwheel?

An elliptical chainwheel is an oval chainwheel. The advantages, if the chainwheel is properly designed, are easier hill climbing and acceleration. The disadvantages are that they are best at one rider position and that too large a change in radius can disturb pedaling rhythm and make the chain more likely to fall off under some conditions.

Freewheels

A. Is there any disadvantage in using extreme jumps in freewheel selection?

Yes. You'll find you're missing a gear somewhere. If you try to get all the gears you want by using an oddly spaced freewheel and the right chainwheels, you'll still miss a gear somewhere, and you'll have a hard-to-remember shifting pattern to boot.

B. Should you replace your chain when you install a new freewheel?

Maybe. Mechanics often say you should do so, and they contend that the old chain will skip on the new freewheel. The reason: the chain and freewheel wear in together. But why not try to skim by with your old chain and see if you can save a few bucks? Be ready to replace the chain, however, if skipping is a problem.

C. What is a fixed gear?

A fixed gear is what a track bike has instead of derailleurs and a freewheel. The bike has only one speed forward so there's no shifting. The bike has no freewheel, so there's no coasting, either. When the bike moves, the cyclist is compelled to pedal. This takes some getting used to.

D. What is the difference between British, French, and Italian threads?

The different kinds of threading are the bicycle industry's Tower of Babel. English threads dominate the industry because many other countries, including Japan, Taiwan, most of Europe, Canada, and the United States, use English threads. French threads, found in bikes manufactured in France, Belgium, Spain, and Switzerland, are not interchangeable with English threads. This noninterchangeability applies to the headset, bottom bracket, pedals, and freewheel. (Other nonthreaded parts, including handlebar stem, seatpost, and crank and wheel axles are also noninterchangeable.) Finally, Italian threads, found on Italian and Mexican bikes, are almost—but not quite—identical to English threads. (Italian threads are cut in a very slightly different shape.) Hence, people often force-fit English threaded components onto Italian frames. (You can get away with that as long as you don't go back and forth between English and Italian threaded components.)

E. *How can I tell if a specific cluster will fit a certain hub? What damage will be done to the hub threads by matching different sizes?*

Find a decent mechanic who has some thread-pitch gauges. If you try to mix Italian with any other kind, you'll ruin the hub. And don't forget, some French bikes come with English-threaded freewheels.

F. *I am apprehensive about taking my freewheel apart. Can I maintain my freewheel without taking it apart?*

Yes, you can. Taking it apart is a tough job that takes lots of time. Instead, just throw the whole thing into a bucket of kerosene. The kerosene will wash unwanted matter out of the bearings and ratchets. Haul the freewheel out, let it dry, and oil it liberally. Let excess oil drip out. That's it.

G. *Why do the cog teeth on some brands of freewheels have special shapes?*

Some of the newer Japanese freewheels are designed so that they are easier for a beginner to shift. The bike sort of snaps from gear to gear, so you don't have to fish for the gear you want.

Gear Changers

A. *What shift levers are best: down tube, stem, or handlebar-end shifters?*

Personal preference is perhaps the best answer to this question. In addition to the above stem shifter placement positions there is a top tube mounting.

Down tube mounting seems to be the safest and simplest position for handlebar shifters. Stem shifters and top tube shifters are a potential danger in the event of an accident (they could dig into your legs). Some riders prefer end shifters and feel more comfortable with that arrangement.

B. What other differences might I find among various kinds of shift levers?

Shift levers come in three styles: ratchet, ratchetless spring-loaded, and friction. They all do the same job—hold the cable in position as the spring in the derailleur is trying to pull at the cable.

Gears and Gearing

A. What is meant by high gear? Low gear?

On a derailleur bicycle with ten or more speeds, these terms are a bit vague, and much more specific terminology is used to refer to each one of the bike's ten gears. But the basic concepts of high gear and low gear are more important than the details of gearing terminology.

When your bike is in high gear, one turn of the pedals makes the bike move further forward that when your bike is in low gear. If the pedals always spin at the same rate, the bike will move faster in high gear than in low gear.

Because the laws of physics say you don't get something for nothing, it's harder to turn the pedals in a high gear. This makes low gear suitable for tough going (uphills, headwinds) and high gear suitable for easy going (downhills, tailwinds).

Your derailleur-equipped bicycle has many gears in between low and high, so you'll always have a gear suitable for the riding conditions that exist at the moment.

B. What are upshift and downshift?

You upshift when you shift into a higher gear. You downshift when you shift into a lower gear.

C. What is meant by gear inches?

Gear inches is the numerical unit of measurement of how high or how low a gear is. Because you shift gears by using different combinations of front chainwheels and rear cogs, you want to be able to compute the gear inches for each chainwheel/cog combination.

The formula for computing gear inches is quite simple:

$$\text{gear inches}: \frac{\text{number of chainwheel teeth}}{\text{number of cog teeth}} \times \text{rear wheel diameter}$$

For example, most 10-speed bikes have a large chainwheel of 52 teeth and a smallest cog of 14 teeth. Rear-wheel diameter is almost always 27 inches. Highest gear, therefore, computes like this:

$$\text{gear inches}: \frac{52}{14} \times 27 = 100$$

How do you interpret a gear-inch number? Different cyclists have their own tastes in gearing, but the following rough guide applies to most cyclists:

Number of gear inches	Use
below 30	climbing steep hills with a heavy load
30 to 40	climbing steep hills with a moderate load or unloaded
40 to 50	climbing moderate hills
50 to 65	climbing gentle hills
65 to 75	cruising on the flats
75 to 85	hard riding on the flats, moderate downhills
85 to 100	down steep hills
above 100	useless to anyone but a well-trained racing cyclist

Why is the gear-inch number used instead of, say, the drive-train ratio (52:14, or 3.7)? The reason is simple: the gear-inch number takes the rear-wheel diameter into account. Sooner or later, you'll want a common frame of reference to compare gear inches on bikes with different wheel diameters. You may want to compare gearing on your 10-speed with gearing on your 26-inch, 3-speed commuting bike, or you may want to compare gearing on a 27-inch 10-speed with gearing on a short person's 24-inch 10-speed.

D. *How do you shift gears?*

On most derailleur-equipped bikes, you shift only while pedaling the bike. As you pedal gently, you move the shift lever. The shift lever communicates with the derailleur via a spring-loaded cable. (Because the cable is spring-loaded, only one cable allows you to move the derailleur in either direction.)

When moved, the derailleur exerts a sideways push on the chain, which derails the chain off the cog or chainwheel it's been sitting on, and hopefully onto the next cog or chainwheel.

Even though you only have to pedal and move the lever to shift your bicycle, it will take you some practice to learn to shift easily. The derailleur doesn't have click-stops, and you have to fish for the right position so the derailleur is centered under the cog you want. If you leave the derailleur halfway between two cogs, you'll get an unnerving grinding noise. Sometimes the derailleur will jump the chain up two or three cogs when you only wanted one.

Derailleurs are a lot like horses—they respond more cooperatively to a confident rider. When you first start using one, it seems like there's a lot to keep track of just to make a simple shift. But you'll soon find it comes naturally.

E. *How do you know what gear you are in?*

Frankly, most cyclists don't know. They have to look down at their drive chain to see what chainwheel/cog combination they last selected. You'll find yourself looking down too, and that's okay, but just don't neglect the more important job of looking ahead for traffic. Eventually, you'll learn either to: (a) remember your gear from the last time you looked, or (b) tell by looking at your shift levers.

F. *How do I take advantage of all ten gears? When do I use which gears?*

It will take you some time and practice to get maximum use out of all your gears. It's worth the effort, though, because you'll find the enjoyment you get out of your bike is many times greater.

When you're very familiar with your bike, you'll find it easy to select the gear you want for existing conditions. One trick you can use to get familiar with your bike more quickly is to write out a gear chart and tape it to the bicycle's handlebar stem or top tube. The chart tells you how many gear inches each of the possible chainwheel/cog combinations delivers. When you consult it regularly, it helps you get a feel for a 60-inch gear, an 80-inch gear, or whatever. When you know how the various gears feel—and where they're located in the shifting pattern—you can shift among them much more adroitly.

To make your gear chart, you first need to count how many teeth are on each of your cogs and chainwheels, and then calculate the gear inches for each possible combination. Write them up in a little chart like this:

	Chainwheels	
	40	52
Cogs	**Gear inches**	
14	77	100
17	64	83
20	54	70
24	45	58
28	39	50

Note: Many bicycles have the exact same gearing shown in this chart.

Your gear chart will eventually wither away and fall off the handlebar stem. But long before it does, you'll have memorized it.

As for when you use which gears, you can use the guide under C as a rough rule. But you should listen to your body more than you listen to any book. When you're cycling most efficiently, you'll be maintaining a swift, smooth pedaling cadence—around 70 revolutions of your pedals per minute—and you'll barely notice any effort required to spin them. Pick a gear ratio which allows you to cycle in this way, and change the gear whenever conditions demand it. When you do that, you'll be making the best possible use of your bicycle's gearing.

Don't fall prey to the beginner's temptation to put the bike in a high gear and slowly grind against the pedals. It will only make you feel tired and sore right away. Many people make the mistaken assumption that this tired feeling proves they're getting better exercise in higher gears. Not so. You get better exercise, ride faster, feel more exhilarated, and get more tired more slowly when you spin lower gears.

G. *How can I shift gears when pedaling uphill?*

Carefully. Practice shifting on the flat for a while beforehand, so you have a good feel for how your derailleurs work. To shift while going uphill, you have to keep several things in mind. You're probably going to be shifting to a larger cog for an easier gear, and if you make such a downshift while you're pushing hard on the pedals you'll put undue strain on your derailleur. But if you don't push on the pedals at all, you'll probably glide to a stop before you have a chance to shift. So you have to strike a fine balance between keeping the bike going and not straining too hard in the midst of a shift. It comes with practice. Don't worry unduly about ruining the bike with beginner's mistakes; it's designed to withstand a few.

Another point about shifting when you pedal uphill is that both your shifting and your pedaling will go smoother if you shift in anticipation of a hill, rather than getting partway up the hill and shifting only after you've lost lots of momentum and cadence.

H. Why can I shift gears on a 10-speed only when moving? I can shift a 3-speed when stopped.

The derailleur shifting mechanism doesn't work unless the chain is moving. This is an inconvenience, but the derailleur has advantages which offset it.

I. What gears do I choose for touring? Racing?

Tourists who carry their own camping gear need extra-low gears to climb hills without getting exhausted. While well-conditioned cyclists can get by with the 39-inch low gear found on most new bikes, they'll suffer a bit for it. A low gear of 25 to 35 inches will make steep hills a lot more palatable.

Most tourists have a high gear of 100 inches or more, but they don't need it. With a 100-inch gear and a cadence of only 80 revolutions per minute, a cyclist travels at 24 miles per hour! That's much faster than any cyclist can cruise on tour. Extra-high gears only allow the tourist to reach dangerously high speeds while going down steep hills. A high gear of 90 inches would allow a tourist to reach 21 miles per hour at a cadence of 80, and 27 miles per hour at the easily achieved cadence of 100.

There are many possible gear combinations for touring, and 12- and 15-speed touring gears are growing in popularity. One good 10-speed touring combination (called a half-step) would look like this:

	Chainwheels	
	42	47
Cogs	**Gear inches**	
14	81	91
17	67	75
21	54	60
26	44	49
32	35	40

Racers have different needs. They're highly trained, so they can make use of high gears; some use gears as high as 119 (53 × 12). Low gears don't do them much good. When a group of racers reaches a steep hill, the good hill climbers in the group force the pace in hopes of dropping the bad hill climbers (who might have other strengths, like sprinting) and thinning out the pack. Therefore, everybody in the pack has to be ready to jump on the hills. Even in the most tortuous uphill stages of the Tour de France, for example, a racer's lowest gear would probably be around 47 (42 × 24). For more gentle inclines, low gears in the high 60s are common. Twelve-speed combinations are used by lots of racers. Today's trend is toward crossover gearing with small "corncob" freewheels and a medium-size chainwheel gap. Here's one example seen on a bike designed for American road races:

	Chainwheels	
	42	52
Cogs	**Gear inches**	
13	87	108
14	81	100
15	76	94
16	71	88
17	67	83
18	63	78

J. Why do they recommend that you don't use the combination of a big front chainwheel with a big rear freewheel cog, or small front chainwheel with a small rear freewheel cog on a 10-speed?

The most-cited reason is that these combinations force the chain to flex so far sideways. They cause a little more wear and tear, and make a little more noise.

A second reason applies only to the big-big combination. Many bicycles are sold with a rear derailleur which is barely adequate to span the difference in chain length required by the various gear combinations. On such a bicycle, the chain may be very tight when in the big-big combination. This tightness exacerbates the wear-and-tear problem.

A third reason applies only to the small-small combination. The chain may be slack in this position, and it may skip on the rear cog. This can sometimes be fixed by adjusting the rear derailleur or by replacing a worn chain or freewheel. The problem always is (or at least should be) fixable.

If you don't have problems with these two combinations, go ahead and use them.

Derailleurs

A. Why does my chain fall off the chainwheels when I shift?
See answer under C, in "Chain."

B. What causes derailleur delay in completing a shift? It takes several complete rotations of the crank before the shift is completed.

There are lots of answers to this question. Some apply only to front or rear derailleurs; others apply to both.

The following answers apply to both:

The derailleur may not be responding promptly to your shift-lever movements. This can be due to dirt in the derailleur's sleeve bearings, a weak spring, rust, physical damage (like a dent), or anything else that prevents free movement. More likely, however, is lack of lubrication in the cable and cable casing leading to the derailleur. The slightest bit of rust inside the casing can make the cable freeze up.

The derailleur may be out of adjustment. If it can't reach quite far enough to make the shift you want it to make, it'll shift slowly, or not at all. You can fix this by tampering with the little set screws which limit the derailleur's range of motion.

A front derailleur may be mounted too high on the frame, or it may be mounted so that its chain cage isn't parallel with the chain. The derailleur should be as low as it can be without hitting the chainwheels. The chain cage may be bent out of shape.

A rear derailleur will work poorly when the chain is old and worn out.

C. How do you choose a derailleur?

Usually, the one that came on the bike is fine. With rare exceptions, front derailleurs are equally suited for any kind of riding. Different rear derailleurs are designed for different purposes, however. Some are suitable only for racing, because they will not accommodate large freewheel cogs or great differences in front chainwheel size. The manufacturers specify which derailleurs are intended for which purposes, and they generally list the freewheel sizes and chainwheel differences for which each derailleur is designed. So if you need to replace your derailleur, you should decide what sort of gearing it's going to be used with. You should restrict your derailleur shopping to models which offer slightly more capacity than you need; derailleurs work better when they're not stretched to their maximum capacity.

D. *Why are there two derailleurs?*

You need two to get all ten speeds. One shifts the front two chainwheels, and one shifts the five rear cogs. You could get as many as seven speeds by using only a rear derailleur, but there would be too much lateral chain bending in some of the speeds.

Maintenance

A. What are the basic tools needed for maintaining my bicycle?

The answer varies somewhat from one bike to the next, so it's impossible to give a specific list of tools for all bicycles. Of course, everyone needs Phillips and regular screwdrivers, small screwdrivers, pliers, and an adjustable wrench. Unfortunately, many beginning mechanics are reluctant to spend money on tools, and they try to skim by with just this small arsenal. That's a mistake, because it's much harder to do a decent job on most maintenance tasks without nonadjustable wrenches. For many tasks, it's virtually impossible.

For most bikes, you'll need wrenches sized from 8 to 12 millimeters, and a second wrench in the 8, 9, or 10 millimeter size may be necessary sometimes. You'll probably need an allen wrench or two. The most commonly used allen wrench sizes are 5 and 6 millimeters, but 4 and 7 millimeter allen wrenches are also needed for some bikes.

You'll also need a pump and tire gauge specially made for the high pressures found in bicycle tires. If you try to get by without them, you'll have more trouble keeping your tires up to snuff. And you'll need a patch kit and tire irons (although you should use your fingers instead of tire irons whenever you can, in order to avoid pinching the tube).

There are many specialty tools for bicycles, and hardly anyone has all of them. One that you should have, however, is a tool for your cotterless crank. This tool allows you to remove the crank for maintenance purposes, but, more important, it allows you to tighten the crank onto the axle. Other specialized tools you may want (and you will need if you take the bike on tour) are a spoke wrench that's the right size for your spoke nipples and a freewheel remover for your brand of freewheel.

B. *Are there monthly maintenance checks I should perform?*

Yes. Of course you should check the tire pressure and chain lubrication. Other things to look for include the headset bearings (they all tend to loosen up), the crank axle bearings, and the spokes. Spokes may get very loose before you notice it, but when they do, you're riding on weaker wheels. A competent wheel-truer should tighten them.

Also make sure that your brakes and derailleurs work well, and that the cables are well lubricated. Check to see that your seat and handlebars haven't loosened up.

C. *Should I lighten my bike?*

Don't spend a lot of money to do so. Expensive parts that save an ounce here and an ounce there aren't worth the money. Most bikes come with parts appropriate to the quality of the frame.

One good investment in light weight you can make, however, is to replace steel rims with aluminum rims. Get lightweight, high-pressure tires to go on your aluminum rims, and the bike will have a light, springy feel you never knew it could deliver.

D. *Can I make my own repairs?*

Certainly. Most good bike mechanics are largely self-taught. To learn how, start by reading a couple of good books on bicycle repair. Find mechanics who know more than you do, and ask them lots of questions. Don't hurry your work. Expect anything to take a long time the first time you try it. And don't attempt a job when you don't have the proper tools.

E. *What kind of lubricants—oils or grease—do you use and for which bicycle parts?*

Ball bearings and cables should be packed in a light grease. Your chain should be oiled. Sleeve bearings should be disassembled and greased if you have the time, or oiled if you don't.

Medical

A. What is meant by bikers' knees, and how can I avoid them?

Chondromalacia (a degeneration of knee cartilages), sprains, strains, and, to a lesser extent, bursitis, are the most frequent knee problems of bicyclists. The two causes of a rider's knee problems are first, not having enough conditioning miles in, so that when the rider starts pushing bigger gears the muscles, ligaments, and tendons will be strong enough to take it, and second, pounding the pedals, not maintaining the same number of revolutions per minute when shifting gears. The key message is to gear down when your knees hurt. High gears increase the stress of pedaling.

B. What would be a good bicycle fitness/training program to follow?

General rules which should be followed by anyone in training for a long-distance ride would be a balanced diet and adequate rest. The training schedule is divided into three general types of training: hard, fast riding (Tuesdays and Thursdays) for muscle strength and aerobic conditioning; long-distance but easier riding on Saturdays for endurance and pacing; and rest or light riding the rest of the week. Keep in mind that hard and easy days should alternate, with one complete rest day per week.

C. What about riding in the city pollution?

Recent studies have shown that a cyclist is less vulnerable to environmental pollutants than car drivers. However, experienced cyclists tend to seek out less-polluted roadways for comfort.

D. What should I eat on long-distance tours?

Of the three major nutrients we extract from foods, the carbohydrates are the most efficient for producing energy over the long haul. When using your muscles and pedaling, it is the carbohydrates that burn for energy. Carbohydrates are stored in the muscles and in the liver in the form of glycogen. In order to prevent depletion of glycogen stores, it is important to eat carbohydrate foods before the ride as well as during the ride. Rice, bread, pancakes, oatmeal, potatoes, bananas, and apples are a few of the high carbohydrate foods. Fat also provides energy during exercise, especially during prolonged exercise such as touring. A normal intake of protein is important for replacing body cells and increasing muscle mass. Protein is not necessary for energy demands, but is important because some amino acids are needed in changing carbohydrate and fat to energy. Before, during, and after riding, adequate amounts of liquids should be consumed. The best beverages are fruit drinks or water.

E. What causes saddle soreness? Will I eventually become hardened against this?

Pain or discomfort caused by the bicycle saddle has two basic causes, pressure and friction. Pressure is responsible for two types of injury which will be referred to as ischial compression and the numb crotch syndrome. Injury caused by friction is called saddle burn or saddle sores. With pressure pain, "toughing it out" by ignoring the pain for long periods can cause severe tenderness and inflammation.

Numerous trials have demonstrated that a slight change in the tilt of the saddle, one or two degrees or perhaps even less, will give almost immediate relief of the pressure pain. Changing the tilt duplicates the natural shifts of position which are part of normal sitting. Individuals who are susceptible to numb crotch must sit back onto the wide part of the saddle. Tilting the front of the saddle down, raising the handlebars, and shortening the distance between the handlebars and saddle all tend to accomplish this.

Saddle burn usually involves only the epidermis. Treatment consists almost entirely of prevention. A lubricant between skin and clothing may be all that is necessary. Once the injury has taken place, the most effective treatment is to stop riding until the inflammation has subsided and healing is complete.

F. What causes leg cramps?

Leg cramps, the kind that come on while riding, are due to overexertion, electrolyte imbalance, or underconditioning. The capacity of muscles improves as they become conditioned by exercise. Cramps are due to overstressing these muscles, often by pushing too-high gears. The treatment is very simple. Get off and walk. Stretch; touch your toes slowly. Next time, don't push so hard. Use lower gears. Drink plenty of fluid on your hard rides. Maintain electrolyte balance with fruit juice.

G. *What causes numb feet?*

Pressure on nerves will cause numbness, as will compression of the blood vessels that supply the nerves. The exact locations of nerves and blood vessels vary slightly among individuals. The straps, the clips, the shoes, or a combination of these may be too tight. Experiment by loosening one at a time, two at a time, or all three until the cause is found, then the problem can be corrected with padding and adjustment of foot position.

H. *What can I do to avoid neck strain?*

The shoulder muscles are the most overworked muscles a bicycle rider has. They support and hold the spine in a position to work and transmit that work to the legs. If the handlebar stem is too short, the shoulder muscles will hurt. If the stem is too long, the arm and neck muscles will hurt. A weight-lifting program to strengthen the arms and shoulders and a change in the position of the seat and handlebars are recommended. You should shift your hand and arm position frequently while riding. Use plenty of padding on the gloves and bars to absorb road shock.

Accessories

A. Lights

1. What effect does a generator have on my tires?

There is little tire wear if the generator is lined up properly and rolls on the tread. When you install the generator the most important thing to watch for is that the rotating axis of the generator drive wheel extends through the center of the rear wheel hub. To keep

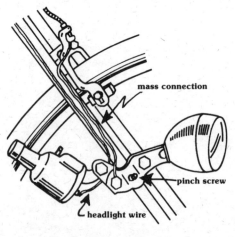

Generator light.

your generator from slipping, and for more traction and less tire wear, install a rubber washer on the generator drive wheel.

2. Which is better, a generator or a battery light?

The ultimate test of any bike light is the amount of light it puts out and the pattern of the beam. Here is a summary of the advantages and the disadvantages of generator and battery lights.

Generator Light

Advantages: Permanently affixed to the bike; always ready to use; cheap to operate and maintain; reliable; unlikely to be tampered with; provides more light than battery light of comparable weight and cost; brightest when you need it most, when riding fast.

Disadvantages: Takes rider's effort to operate; can't be used separately from the bike; provides no light when standing still (unless equipped with auxiliary battery power).

Battery Light

Advantages: Does not require rider's effort to operate; some models can be used away from bike to double as flashlight; works even when the bike is not moving.

Disadvantages: As a rule, not permanently affixed to the bike; often not there when you need it; expensive to operate and maintain; less reliable; batteries often deteriorate when not in use; easily tampered with if left on bike; provides less light than generator light of comparable weight and cost; cheap battery lights are too dim to be useful.

3. Do you wear the flashing beacon taillight units on your body or on your bike?

There are several flashing beacon taillight units on the market today. These flashing lights are bright and visible. They work in the same manner as a strobe light, flashing short, intense beams at intervals of from 40 to 90 times per minute. Most states require that they be mounted on the bike, if this is your only taillight. If you have a regular reflector or taillight on the bike, you can wear the flashing lights on your body.

4. What should I look for in a lighting system?

The headlight should have either a big diameter or a rectangular shape, to be seen from the front. The lens should be the fresnel type (the kind that looks corrugated rather than smooth) to produce the best beam pattern. The taillight should also be big. The lens should not be smooth on the inside but should have an intricate pattern of small angled surfaces, like a good reflector. Unless your state law requires red, you should opt for amber which is more visible.

B. Clothing and Apparel

1. Why do cyclists wear cycling shorts?

There are several advantages to riding with cycling shorts. Because of their snug fit, they move with your legs as you pedal. Good-quality shorts have a soft leather insert in the crotch. It serves as a liner which cushions the body and absorbs perspiration and thus decreases friction potential. Reinforced seats are also beneficial, for they add extra padding and increase comfort.

2. Do I need cycling shoes? Cleats?

If you are at the stage where you want to take longer rides, you should start thinking about getting cycling shoes. They slide in and out of your straps easily, and the soles are strong enough to withstand constant foot pressure. Don't attach cleats unless you are interested in long-distance traveling. Cleats are not practical for getting on and off your bike frequently and are unsuitable for walking.

3. Should cyclists wear glasses?

Yes. Glasses protect the eyes from flying objects and excessive sunlight. A word about sunlight is in order. When the eyes are exposed for several hours to bright light, such as summer sunlight, the visual pigments in the retina are washed out, and the eyes function poorly when darkness falls. For this reason, sunglasses are a good idea for any long rides during the day, even if the sun is not uncomfortably bright.

4. Are rear-view mirrors that attach to glasses or helmets a good idea?

Rear-view mirrors allow you to spot approaching traffic before you can hear its approach. Mirrors mounted on glasses, helmets, or caps are effective because you can tilt your head to see in desired direction.

5. Cycling clothing is expensive. What can I wear as a substitute?

A biker's uniform consists of chamois-lined shorts, jersey, helmet/cap, sunglasses, leg and arm warmers, and shoes. If you're not ready to make the investment, here are a few things you should know. Light weight is important, for you don't want to carry around any more weight than you have to. Clothing should be streamlined so that it doesn't flap around in the wind and get in your way or slow you down. Clothing fabrics should breathe and ventilate. For convenience, clothing that can be machine washed and dried is good. Generally speaking, it is better to choose a natural fiber than a synthetic fiber for bicycling. Wool is the best choice. Knits are soft and comfortable and give with body movements. Shorts should have few seams and should be flat to avoid chafing. T-shirts are functional. Paper-thin nylon windbreakers are a good top layer. Long johns can be used for cold-weather riding, but have the minor disadvantage of being cotton instead of wool. A good noncycling shoe for cycling is narrow and trim, and as firm as possible.

C. Miscellaneous

1. Why do many cyclists choose not to use a kickstand?

Kickstands weigh a lot, and the bike falls over anyway. Far better to lean the bike up against a building or shackle it to a signpost.

2. Why do most new bikes come without chainguards? They keep your clothing from getting caught in the chain.

Rubber bands and pants clips do the job better. Chainguards have a way of rattling loose and becoming maintenance headaches. Chainguards on 10-speed bikes are unsatisfactory compromises which have lots of maintenance problems and also don't do the job well.

3. Why do new bikes come without fenders?

Fenders are cumbersome, and they add to the bicycle's weight and maintenance problems. But they're genuinely useful, and the real reason bikes don't have them is so the bikes will look more like professional racing bikes. So for reasons of style, fenders are unpopular.

Accidents and Safe Riding

A. Which side of the street should cyclists ride on?

Ride on the right, with traffic. Every accident survey and every analysis of traffic engineering data proves that riding on the left is lethal.

B. Which rules of the road apply to cyclists?

Virtually all of them. Rules differ from one state to the next, but cyclists in all states are expected to follow commonsense rules. Among these are: stopping at traffic lights and stop signs; signaling turns; staying to the right when traveling more slowly than other traffic; using lights after dark; and not swerving into the path of overtaking or oncoming traffic.

C. Why should I wear a bicycle helmet? I don't race.

You probably think you don't need a helmet because you don't ride very fast. But it's quite possible for you to crack your skull while cycling at walking speed just by falling off your bike and hitting your head on the ground. Even if you don't crack your skull, any blow to the head is likely to produce a painful concussion. Helmets made for cycling are lightweight, well ventilated, and comfortable. They shield your head from the sun and help keep you cool on a hot day. You can't afford not to have the protection they provide.

D. What is the safest way to brake in wet weather?

Brake carefully. You have to cycle more slowly to begin with, and you should apply your brakes early so they have a chance to squeegee the water from the rim. At this point, the brakes can begin to slow the bike down. But you have less traction between your tires and the wet road, so it's easier to make the bike skid. Don't squeeze the brake handles too hard, and you'll slowly come to a safe stop.

E. How do most cycling accidents occur?

Most cycling accidents occur as a result of the cyclist committing gross violations—running stoplights, swerving out of side streets in the face of traffic, cycling on the wrong (left) side of the road, cycling at night without a light or reflectors, and carrying passengers or unsecured cargo.

Losing control and falling off the bike figure significantly. Most bicycle accidents do not involve automobiles, although automobiles are a major factor in serious bicycle accidents.

The most common cause of serious motorist-fault bicycle accidents is overtaking and colliding with a cyclist from behind. Drunkenness, dusk, and narrow roads figure heavily in this kind of accident; this suggests the importance of dressing to be noticed when you cycle.

In addition, many cyclists become accident victims because they fail to anticipate common motorist errors. When motorists make these errors, a cyclist must be ready to take evasive action without hesitation.

F. What can I do to be more noticeable?

Do a lot. Wear a helmet; any cyclist who does will tell you the helmet attracts attention and commands respect. Wear brightly colored clothing such as a yellow windbreaker. Don't ever wear dark clothing when you cycle. Festoon your bicycle with reflective tape, in addition to the usual complement of reflectors. Wear fluorescent-colored pants-cuff clips, even when you have short pants on. Wear a reflective vest. All these things enhance what the government calls your conspicuity.

G. What can I do to be safe cycling at night?

Wear all the bright, conspicuous clothing you can dig up, and dress your bike accordingly. Get a bright, attention-getting light, visible from both front and rear; many wise cyclists use more than one light so they're conspicuous from every angle.

Now take a mental tour of your perimeter. Do you have a substantial amount of reflective material visible from every angle? Do you have a light visible from every angle? If the answer is no, consider yourself invisible and unsafe at night.

You may want a headlight to help you see in addition to lights to help you be seen. But don't mistake one for the other; a headlight alone doesn't do much to help you be seen. When selecting a headlight, avoid the cheaper department-store models. Go to a bike shop, and invest in a top-quality light that's bright enough and reliable enough to do you some good.

Frequently Asked Questions

H. *What other safety equipment is important?*
  Gloves protect your hands in case of a fall. A warning device—a small horn, or in states where it's legal, a whistle—is important. A bell is not an adequate warning device.

Storage and Theft

A. *What is the best way to lock a bike?*
  A bike isn't like a car. It doesn't have a steel skin to protect its valuable components from pilfering or tampering. Many cyclists like to carry a pump, tool kit, and saddlebag; these items are always vulnerable on an exposed bike.
  Accordingly, the best way to secure a bike is to enclose it. Several companies manufacture bicycle lockers, and these lockers are slowly finding their way into parking lots at schools, employment areas, and train stations. Another way to enclose a bike is to have a supervised storage area. Supervised storage can make use of existing space within a building, providing secured bicycle parking without the need for lockers. Supervision can be worked into existing security or receptionist job descriptions, so no additional personnel are necessary.
  The second-best way to secure a bike is to lock each of its most valuable and tempting pieces individually—both wheels and the frame. There are several ways to do this.

B. *What kinds of locking devices are available?*
  The old-fashioned way to lock a bike is to pass a 4-foot length of case-hardened chain through both wheels and the frame and around a signpost, and secure the whole package with a strong padlock. A chain like this is vulnerable to the bicycle thief's bolt cutters.
  Several popular brands of high-security bike locks use a U-shaped device just big enough to go around the frame, rear wheel, and a signpost. The cyclist may remove the front wheel and slip it in the tight little package of locked-up components. The entire lock weighs around two pounds. Locks like this take so long for a thief to break open that they can be regarded as secure—but parts on the bike are still exposed.

Some manufacturers offer high-security bike racks. The cyclist rolls the bicycle into its berth and uses only his own padlock to snare the bicycle—and both its wheels—in the rack. The question of parts and accessories remains unresolved.

Locking cables are an alternative to chains. Thick cables are harder to cut open than chains.

C. *Is theft insurance available?*

Yes. You can get it as part of your homeowner's policy (often as an extra-cost rider; ask your agent for details) or as a separate policy. Manufacturers of U-shaped locks offer insurance if a bike is stolen while it is protected with the lock.

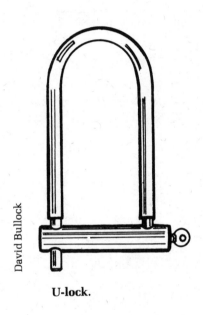

U-lock.

Bike Business

A. *I'm interested in opening a bike shop. How do I go about this?*
Contact the following:

Bicycle Manufacturers Association of America
1101 Fifteenth Street NW
Washington, DC 20005

National Bicycle Dealers Association
435 North Michigan Avenue
The Tribune Tower
Chicago, IL 60611

B. *I would like to become a bicycle mechanic. Can I go to school to learn the trade?*
Raleigh and Schwinn operate the two professional bicycle mechanics programs in the United States. You must be affiliated with a company in order to enter its school. Check your local junior college, night school, and extension programs for offerings of a mechanics program. Try to get an apprentice-type job at a local bike shop.

Legislation

A. *Many bicyclists are campaigning against bikeways. Why?*
A controversy has prevailed for a long time between the advocates of the separate bikeway versus the advocates of the shared highway. Antibikeway reasoning is this: separate bikeways are not usually designed with the attributes most needed by cyclists; they are unsafe at speed and impractical for the more experienced riders. Designers often ignore the fact that bicyclists are also commuters looking for the shortest routes from here to there. Unfortunately, many routes go nowhere in particular.

B. *I've heard something about converting unused railroad tracks to bikeways. Is this really being done?*
An intriguing form of bicycle transportation, once very popular in America, is the railbike. Very simply, the railbike is a regular bike fitted with special attachments so that it can be ridden on rails.

Today the Bureau of Outdoor Recreation estimates that there are well over 10 thousand miles of unused railroad track in America; as more lines fold, unused track will increase. Should these tracks be pulled up, at great expense, or is there a better solution? Some people believe they have found the solution: the reintroduction of the railbike on unused and little-used track. William J. Gillum, president of the American Railbike Association and proponent of widespread railbike use, believes the time has come for the rediscovery of an old idea.

C. *How can we get a bikeway in our town?*

First you must convince an elected official that a bikeway is needed in your town. Approach him with presurveyed routes, and convince him that a bikeway will provide safe access for cycling commuters, fun and recreation for others. Next, you must take the necessary steps to get on the agenda for a meeting with city or town councilmen. Be prepared with maps or slides depicting the route, and submit your proposal in writing. Include a full budget and time schedule taking the project from start to finish. Get newspaper support by showing the many problems existing for both motorists and cyclists. Have about 15 concerned supporters converge on the meeting and be sure to have your sponsoring official well informed of the entire proposal so that he can actively give support at the meeting.

D. *Why should a cyclist support bottle bill legislation?*

In states which have bottle bill legislation, highway litter (glass) has been noticably reduced. The best thing to do is to write to your congressman and senators. Further information is available from:

Ralph Hirsch, Legislative Chairman for the League
   of American Wheelmen
112 South Sixteenth Street, 9th floor
Philadelphia, PA 19102

Touring

A. How do I start a bike club?

Start with a handful of cyclists, and offer membership to anyone of any age who can ride responsibly. To drum up support, spread handouts and posters all over your area; in schools, supermarkets, the downtown business district, and bike shops, announcing the starting of the club. At the initial meeting schedule a ride for the following weekend. Your next meeting should be organizational and should include such topics as: name, objectives, type of membership, amount of dues, and temporary chairman and secretary. If regularly scheduled rides are your main purpose, a committee should be formed to plan these rides well in advance and to see that the schedule is published and sent to all members. Post the schedule in local bike shops and on college campuses to invite new riders. Also, each ride should be led by a ride captain. If you plan to promote a race, a rally, or even an interclub ride, committees should be established for these purposes. You may want a committee to be responsible for social events, such as summer picnics, a Christmas party, and awards ceremonies.

B. Who do I contact for maps for bicycle touring?

Write to your county and state highway departments, Department of Recreation, or United States Geological Survey, and inquire at local bike shops and bike clubs.

C. I want to get started in touring, but I don't want to go it alone. Are there organized tours I can join?

There are more than 30 organizations around the country that provide planned tours for the novice and veteran cyclist. There are a variety of offerings, ranging from easy riding to real challenges. Check the pages of *Bicycling* magazine for tour offerings, or write to

Bicycling magazine for a reprint of "Group Tours: More Than Thirty to Choose From."

D. *Am I allowed to carry a bicycle on a train? Airplane? Bus?*

Amtrak has announced that folding bicycles can be taken without charge on all of its passenger trains. Regular bikes will be accepted, for a $2 handling fee, only on trains that have baggage cars, regardless of trip length. The loading and unloading has to be done by the railroad's freight handlers. Unfortunately, many Amtrak trains do not have baggage cars or baggage-handling service. Inquire about services before you plan train travel.

Almost all domestic airlines now charge a $10 or $12 fee to handle bicycles. The bikes must be either packed in a cardboard carton or have the handlebars loosened and turned sideways and the pedals removed. Some airlines require protruding parts to be packed with foam rubber or some similar substance. The bicycle is not part of the allowable free baggage. Each carrier has exceptions to the rule. Always check with your individual carrier before you plan air travel. Bicycles are generally included in the baggage allowance on international flights.

Greyhound will accept bicycles. They can be carried as one of three pieces of baggage, and there is no extra charge. However, they must be packed in a bicycle box, and there is the possibility that the bicycle will not arrive on the same bus as you will. To overcome this possibility, you could buy your ticket ahead of time and have the bicycle shipped to your destination to await your arrival.

E. *Is it practical to take my bicycle with me for touring abroad, or should I rent a bike or buy one over there?*

Take a well-broken-in bicycle along. You save the purchase taxes, and store prices are about as high as in the United States, so the total price may be higher due to the taxes.

F. *Are automobile bicycle racks safe?*

Yes, if you follow a simple checklist in determining what kind of rack is most suitable for your needs. Consider mounting; do you want a carrier that attaches to the car roof, the bumper, or the trunk lid? Will the rack fit your car, and will your bike fit the rack? How many bikes do you need to transport? There are models available to fit all needs. Contact your local bike shop dealer for assistance.

G. *What should I know about packing for a tour?*

Don't carry anything you can leave behind, and don't leave behind anything you may really need (like tools or first-aid items). Your load must be absolutely secure so it doesn't shift or bounce. You should strive to meet three objectives:

1. The load should be as low as possible.
2. As much of your load should be between the axles as possible.
3. The load must be well balanced.

To keep the load low, put heavy objects in the bottom of your pannier bags. Consider getting an in-frame bag for heavy items like tools. But by all means, balance your load with an amply stuffed handlebar bag and/or front panniers. Before you start packing for your tour, pick up your bike by the top tube and note where the center of gravity is. When the bike is fully loaded, the center of gravity should be in the same place. If you don't balance your touring load, you may get dangerous steering shimmy.

David Knox

Bike packing.

H. *How do I handle a bicycle loaded with touring gear?*

There's no special trick to cycling with a full load of bike-camping gear. You'll get the feel of it soon enough, but there are a few things to expect. A slight wobble or unsteady ride will tell you if the load is not even. Ease your grip on the handlebars for a short downhill stretch, and feel how the bike wants to go. Gearing and daily mileage are two major adjustments. Both have to be lowered. Be much more cautious—you new pack mule is hard to control.

I. How can I take the kids along?

It takes longer to prepare for a trip if you plan to take the children, but the extra time can be well spent. First, you must decide if a long bike tour with the children is possible. Consider their health, mental attitudes, and known travel experiences. Another primary decision is what type of bikes to get for the children. There are several options: their own bike, if old enough; bike carriers; or a bike buggy if younger. Get acquainted with the bikes, and begin a conditioning program. The main disadvantage to having the children along is that everything must be geared to their level which can produce a strain on the adults. It can also be hard at times to motivate children to accomplish what must be done. Patience and careful preparation should pull you through.

J. Will baggage get caught in my spokes?

Not if you're careful. Rear panniers are the basic bulk-carrying bags used in bike touring. When selecting a pair, affix them to your bike, fully loaded, to be sure they do not interfere with the wheel or derailleur or with your feet. They should be well anchored on a rack bolted to the frame below the saddle and on or near the dropouts. Molded plastic or fiberboard stiffeners can help hold the bags away from the wheel. If the bags are deep enough to reach your feet or pedals, be sure they are tapered to allow clearance.

K. What is the TransAmerica Trail?

The TransAmerica Trail is a 4,325-mile-long continental crossing. (The trail seems to change in length from year to year; this was the length in 1978.) The trail offers a view of a different America, it is not the America that is seen from the interstate highways. The view from both sides of the trail is that of a rural, small-town country, containing a rich diversity of land and people. When planning the route, emphasis was placed on varied and scenic terrain; it avoids long stretches with no services, such as deserts; and the most direct routes between two places are often not used because of high traffic density. The trail begins (or ends) in Oregon and winds up in Virginia.

Bikecentennial, a nonprofit service organization for touring cyclists, was chartered for the express purpose of developing the TransAmerica Bicycle Trail, and to operate organized trips on that route as a dual celebration of the American Bicentennial and the introduction of the bicycle to the United States in 1876.

Racing

A. I'm interested in bicycle racing. Who do I contact?

The United States Cycling Federation is the governing body of the sport of bicycle racing in the United States. All bicycle racing clubs in the United States are members. This organization licenses racers. For information write to:

United States Cycling Federation
Box 669, Wall Street Station
New York, NY 10005

B. What is a velodrome?

A velodrome is a bicycle racing track. Aside from the general oval shape, there is an infinite variety in the characteristics of tracks. They can be outdoor or indoor or a little bit of both; asphalt, wood, cement, or clay; 140 meters to over a kilometer around; wide enough for car racing or no wider than three bikes; varying in banking from virtually level to 60 degrees.

C. What is the design of a typical track bike?

Track racing requires special techniques and a special bike. While track bikes have the same general outlines as road bikes, they are quite different. The utmost in responsiveness is required, therefore all concessions to soft-riding comfort are forgotten. The frame is as upright as possible. All track bikes are built for maximum rigidity and lightness. The majority of track bikes weigh around 17 pounds. This weight is saved in a number of ways. There is just one gear, so the chain is shorter. There's one chainwheel in front, one cog in back, and there's no derailleur. The drive is direct; pedal forward, you go forward; pedal backward, you go backward. There is no freewheel. There are no brakes, either. Fewer-spoked wheels, lighter pedals, lighter saddle, and lighter tires save on weight.

D. Who is Eddy Merckx?
Merckx is a super-rider. He was born in southern Belgium on June 17, 1945. He is 5 feet, 9 inches tall. His first title was the National Amateur Championship of Belgium in 1962. His first world championship was the amateur road race of 1964. He turned pro in 1965 and was second in the Belgian National Pro Championship that year. His first "classic" victory was the Milan-San Remo of 1966. In 1966 he took the championship of Flanders. He won the World Professional Road Championship in 1967. He has won several Tours de France and several Giri d'Italia. His victory in the 1969 "Super Prestige Pernod," the European pros' all-rounder competition, included a record number of points. He has won several Six-Day races at Ghent, Charleroi. His record speeds for the Milan-San Remo, the Tour of Belgium, and the Grande Prix de Lugano still stand. He holds the world hour record. Part of Eddy Merckx's mystique is in his incredibly successful season in the year 1971. In this year he won four Classics, the World Championship, and every stage race in which he rode.

E. What cycling training books can you recommend so that I can follow a program on my own?
Buy a copy of *Cycling*, published by C.O.N.I.–Central Sports School–F.I.A.C., Rome, Italy (1972). This book should be available at any good cycle shop. Also, *Get Fit with Bicycling*, by the editors of *Bicycling* magazine.

F. What is roller riding?
Rollers are a kind of a treadmill you can use to cycle without going anywhere. For bicyclists not familiar with rollers, they are simply three revolving cylinders contained by a frame. The two rear rollers cradle the bicycle's rear wheel, while the front wheel rests on the front roller. An elastic belt between the front and middle rollers makes all three revolve simultaneously when activated by the bicycle's wheels.

G. How does roller riding benefit me?
Roller riding will help you to better handle a bike. You become a much smoother rider on the road after learning to ride high rpm's on rollers. Rollers will naturally develop a smooth, circular-type pedaling, because if you don't ride straight on rollers, you'll come off. Rather than lunging down on each pedal, you get a much more even power drive using a full pedal stroke. Rollers also provide effective exercise which benefits the cardiovascular and respiratory systems.

H. Is it true that swimming and cycling don't mix? How about jogging?

The only thing wrong with sports other than cycling is that there are only so many hours in a day. Every hour spent swimming or running is one less hour spent riding. Swimming will not hurt cycling; running will help it some; but the best training is just to get on your bike and ride as much as possible.

I. *Do training camps exist?*

For information on training camps, contact the United States Cycling Federation. (See address under A.) Also, check the pages of *Velo-news*, a journal of bicycle racing, Box 1257, Brattleboro, VT 05301.

J. *Why is the Tour de France such a famous race?*

For the French, the Italians, the Germans, the Belgians, and the Swiss, the Tour de France is truly the "greatest show on earth." It is a show with hundreds of actors and thousands of spectacular sets. Its stage is the heart of Europe, from the peaks of Chartreuse and the Massif Central to the plains of the North. It passes through great cities and countless picturesque villages. It is a three-week run with thousands of extras—some 8 hundred reporters, a score of doctors, nurses, trainers, and representatives of commercial sponsors who, day after day, follow the cyclists in hundreds of vehicles of all descriptions. It is a fabulous extravaganza, rich in human conflicts and tragedies, watched by 15 million spectators who, enthralled, crowd along the roads, not to mention many millions more glued to their TV sets, who see "live" the daily drama as it unfolds.

K. *Please define some of the basic racing terminology.*

Criterium: a road race over a short closed course for many laps. Lap is usually less than one mile on city streets.

Cyclo-cross: this type of racing almost always takes place on an under-two-mile circuit filled with obstacles such as streams, plowed fields, staircases, or hurdles, that require the rider to frequently dismount and run with the bike on his shoulder.

Handicap race: a race in which weaker riders are given a time or distance handicap over the stronger riders. In theory all contestants will finish together in a perfectly handicapped race. Track handicaps are generally in distance; road handicaps in time.

Madison: several teams of two cyclists each compete in this event. Partners spell each other by slinging each other into the race every few laps.

Mass-start race: any race in which all the riders start together. Most road races are run in this manner.

Match race: a race in which two or three riders ride for a short distance (1,000 meters or less) in a match of sprinting ability. This race demands high technical ability on the part of the rider and considerable "racing sense."

Miss and out race: a track race in which all riders start together and at the end of each lap the last one or two riders are withdrawn from the field until there are only three riders remaining; the race continues with a free lap and then a final sprint lap to determine first, second, and third place.

Motor-pace or "demi-fond": this form of track racing is very popular in Europe and a World Championship event. Riders use a special bike with a small front wheel to ride closely behind motorcycles driven by pacers who stand erect to give maximum shelter. Speeds usually vary from 40 to 60 miles per hour.

Point race: a track (or sometimes criterium) race in which points are awarded to leaders on various laps. The winner is the finisher with the highest point total. In bicycle racing, point awards are usually given to the first five places on the basis of 7-5-3-2-1.

Pursuit race: a track race in which two riders or teams start at opposite positions on the course and race to catch each other. The winner is the rider or team catching the other or the one in the lead after a designated distance.

Road race: a race run over open highways, preferably with a variety of terrain.

Time trial: any race, road or track, in which the individual rider or team of riders competes against the clock. Stage racing is the same as road racing, only repeated day after day. The Tour de France, at three weeks, is the longest of these.

Track race: a race run over a specially constructed track (velodrome) with a smooth surface (usually cement, asphalt, or wood). Most tracks are ¼ mile or less per lap and have steeply banked turns so that riders may maintain high speeds.

Odds and Ends

A. *What is the address for the President's Council on Fitness and Sports?*

President's Council on Physical Fitness and Sports
C. Carson Conrad, Executive Director
Donohoe Building, Suite 3030
400 Sixth Street, SW
Washington, DC 20201

B. *What is the IHPVA?*

The International Human Powered Vehicle Association; a non-profit organization dedicated to promoting improvement, innovation, and creativity in the design and development of human powered vehicles, as well as encouraging public interest in physical fitness and good health through exercise.

IHPVA
c/o C. R. Kyle/Engineering
California State University
Long Beach, CA 90840

C. *How can I find out which colleges offer cycling as an intercollegiate sport?*

Write to:

National Association of Intercollegiate Athletics
1221 Baltimore Avenue
Kansas City, MO 64105

D. *What are the Gossamer Condor and the Gossamer Albatross?*

The Gossamer Condor is a pedal-powered airplane. It is the first of its kind to stay aloft for more than five minutes and the first to make 180-degree turns successfully. It weighs 70 pounds and has a wing span of 96 feet. It was the first time in history that maneuvers had been possible in human-powered flight. The aircraft's designer, Dr. Paul MacCready, designed a new craft, the Gossamer Albatross, which flew across the 22-mile English Channel. The overall weight was reduced from 70 to 55 pounds. The craft averaged an altitude of around 15 feet.

Gossamer Condor.

E. *What is a recumbent bicycle?*

A bicycle in which the rider assumes a prone position, designed to reduce wind drag.

F. *Are bicycles available for the handicapped?*

People with many sorts of handicaps can enjoy the sport of bicycling. One such cyclist is Robert C. Dean, Jr., an amputee who bicycles with an above-the-knee prosthesis. Says Dean, "Given the will and with a few simple bicycle modifications, there is no fundamental reason why a one-legged person cannot ride a bicycle as long as his good leg is reasonably competent." For a person with the use of only one hand, special hand controls and levers can be installed. There are hand-cranked tricycles for paraplegics available from a number of custom builders. Tandem cycling has been enjoyed by blind cyclists with a partner who can see to steer the way.

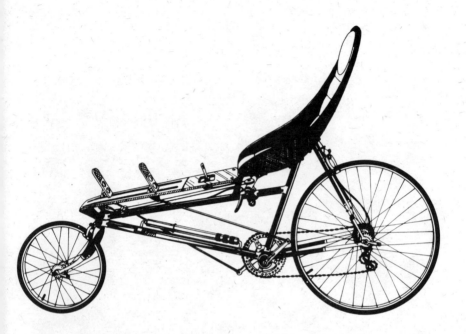

Wilson recumbent (reclining) bicycle.

Mike Piper

Hand-cranked tricycle.